W9-BGK-838

SENIOR HIGH VOL. 2
Pacesetter

The Complete Youth Ministry Resource

Inside The Church

FINDING YOUR PLACE WITHIN GOD'S FAMILY

■

David C. Cook Publishing Co.

Elgin, Illinois/Weston, Ontario

Senior High PACESETTER

■

INSIDE THE CHURCH
Finding Your Place within God's Family

DAVID C. COOK PUBLISHING CO.
Elgin, Illinois/Weston, Ontario
INSIDE THE CHURCH
Finding Your Place within God's Family
© 1986 David C. Cook Publishing Co. All rights reserved. Except where noted otherwise in the text, no part of this publication may be reproduced without permission of the publisher.

■

Creative Team

Project Editor: Kevin A. Miller
Editors: Anne E. Dinnan; Paul N. Woods
Assistant Editor: Eric Potter
Designer: Jill Novak

■

Management Team

David C. Cook III, Editor in Chief
Joseph Bayly, President
Ralph Gates, Director of Church Resources
Marlene D. LeFever, Executive Editor of Ministry Resources
Jim Townsend, Bible Editor
Gregory Eaton Clark, Director of Design Services

■

Scripture quotations, unless otherwise noted, are from the *Holy Bible: New International Version.* © 1978 New York International Bible Society. Used by permission of Zondervan Bible Publishers.

Topic introduction by Gary W. Downing

We'd like to thank the many encouragers who helped PACESETTER become reality. —The Editors

Published by David C. Cook Publishing Co.
850 North Grove Avenue
Elgin, IL 60120
Cable address: DCCOOK
Second printing, October 1986
Printed in the United States of America
Library of Congress Catalog Card Number: 85-72934
ISBN: 0-89191-325-4

Cover photo by Bakstad Photographics

Inside The Church

FINDING YOUR PLACE WITHIN GOD'S FAMILY

*I*n a recent poll published in *USA Today,* attending religious services ranked fourth on the list of things teens *don't* like to do. That's ahead of going to school, which ranked sixth! Many teenagers have a hard time seeing that there is a place in the church for them. The experience many teenagers have as Christians gather for worship and nurture, is that the church is only for grown-ups or little kids. Worship is geared to adults. Sunday school is directed toward children. And high school kids fit neither category.

As a result, teenagers often feel a sense of alienation, rejection, apathy, or outright anger: "Church is boring!" "None of my friends go." "Sunday school is for simpletons." "It's all stupid!" Phrases like these probably mask the underlying feelings that they just don't belong. Church is not for them. How can we help turn that around?

It won't be easy. But we can help pave the way for teenagers to find a place in the church. Start by analyzing some of the barriers a teenager might encounter walking in the front door of the church on a Sunday morning. And start working on those barriers. Are there some things you can begin to change—even in little ways—that might help create an environment of hospitality for teenagers?

You can be a vital link in changing how the church views and responds to young people—and in how they respond to the church. There *is* a place in the church for teenagers. Let's make those places happen!

INSIDE ● THIS ● VOLUME

Inside the Church (Volume Two in the PACESETTER series) can help you lead your kids to discover and enjoy their places within the church.

First, for background on the topic and your own enrichment, we offer you "Expert Insights," articles by leaders in youth ministry. For example, how *do* you involve kids in the church? And should you? Check out the article by veteran youth minister Jim Hancock. Steve Board, former editor of *Eternity* magazine, wrestles with the very human problems in every church. And youth minister Ridge Burns looks at ways to minister to kids who have grown up in the church—*and* reach kids outside.

Then, use PACESETTER's practical programming tools:

■ The "Meetings" section gives you five complete meeting plans on church-related topics. Reproduce the activity pieces at the back of this book for use with these meetings.

■ In the "More Bright Ideas" section, you'll find around 20 activity ideas, many suitable as meetings in themselves. Use these ideas whenever you need them.

■ Need material for an upcoming retreat? You'll find it in "Breakaway": an engaging lock-in on the theme, "Finding My Place in God's Family."

■ Need a fun, easy-to-perform drama for a youth night or service that's almost here? Turn to the "Kids in the Spotlight" section for the humorous sketch, "As the Church Turns."

■ Finally, to help you build a solid, caring youth group, we've included a section called, "Nurturing Your Group."

So if you're looking at a blank calendar and wondering what you're going to do, you've come to the right place. Whether you need one activity or months of programs, PACESETTER is at your service. □

Contents

Contents

A veteran youth worker asks pointed questions about involving youth in the church.

Involving Kids in the Church:

Potential and Problems

Let's admit we have a problem. We are possessed of a vague and, we think, virtuous intent to get adolescents involved—we mean really involved—in the life of the church.

Trouble is, we don't know, or can't agree, on what that means. Much of our talk about involving adolescents in congregational life is little more than wishful thinking. We have yet to effectively "philosophize" on the subject, so we settle for a Youth Sunday here and a workday there until we can find time to think it through. Meanwhile, most adolescents remain outsiders and are not truly involved in congregational life.

BY JIM HANCOCK

Illustration by Roger T. De Muth

The Big Question: What Is Involvement?

What do we mean when we talk of *involvement* in the church? The water is shallow and muddy at this bend in the creek. For some it means putting kids on the ruling boards of the congregation— whether or not they vote is a bone of contention. For others, involvement means providing (sometimes manufacturing) opportunities for adolescents to be in front of the congregation. For yet another group, kids are a sort of garbage detail: ''That sounds like a good job for the youth group.''

What *do* we mean by ''involvement''? The Big Question falls neatly in two, like the halves of a peanut:

1. Who are kids? Which is to say, ''Who are the people we want to involve; what are they like?'' And,
2. Why do we want to involve them in the church? Or, ''What is the aim of involvement; what do we hope to produce?''

When we've satisfied these lesser inquiries, the Big Question may well begin to answer itself.

1. WHO ARE KIDS?

A 16-year-old boy walks stiffly from the throne-sized pastor's chair to the oaken pulpit. For a moment his gaze is captured by the backside of the rostrum, a concave affair which he never had occasion to imagine till now. A glass of water, a hymnal shoved far into the shelf beneath the lectern, a clock set at a slant so the preacher can track his progress, a little plaque that reads, ''Feed My Sheep''; each object in its turn grabs a tiny fraction of his attention. His palms reach toward two spots on the outside rail, spots rubbed smooth by the oil of preachers' hands. The boy's fingers don't quite fit the dark places on the wood—like his stiff corduroy sport coat doesn't quite fit his narrow shoulders. Perhaps he will grow into both.

Right now he is nervous to the point of distraction. Glancing at the clock he has no idea how many seconds have ticked by while he stood there, silent. His saliva turns to dust, his breath catches in his throat; he does not know whether he will pass out after he reads the call to worship or just pass out. And in the second pew, center, an old woman smiles.

Surely that scene has been repeated more times than there are pulpits in America, and with varied results. Sometimes the old woman's smile is turned to tears of joy—the future of the church is secure. Sometimes she shakes her tired head and wonders . . .

Is Youth Sunday a rite of passage? Or is it more a nuisance, a curiosity, like a sweater on a dog? Is it amateur night at the church, a sort of audition from which an occasional bright hope rises?

all, produce visibility for the youth of the church. But what's right about them? Are they an appropriate expression of involvement for kids?

The trainers at the San Diego Zoo used to make a big deal about not teaching the animals unnatural tricks. They seemed concerned about the integrity of the sea lions and big cats they worked with. It sounded good to me: Let cats act like cats. They don't talk about that at the zoo these days, but I still think about that bit of early 70's conscience when folks talk about Youth Sunday. I wonder, "Who is this for?" Not that kids shouldn't extend themselves for the benefit of the larger church—but what sort of extension will be most meaningful; what will nurture the integrity of kids and adults? Who are those kids anyway?

Advance Men on Campus

■

As far as the church is concerned, I propose this answer: Christian kids are the representatives of Christ in their world. As surely as insurance salesmen present Christ to their co-workers and clients, as certainly

speak into the microphone. But they are indispensable in the wearing of tennis shoes and sandals and speaking the truth to 15-year-olds. "How can they hear without someone preaching to them? And how can they preach unless they are sent? As it is written, 'How beautiful are the Nikes of those who bring good news!' " (Romans 10:14, 15, sort of). Who's going to preach the Gospel to high school students? Not me; I'm not allowed on campus. The Good News will be carried to high school by high school students.

That fact alone legitimizes the nurture of kids in the church. All that specialized attention—the budget, the staff, the Kool-Aid stains on the carpet—are worth it because the Gospel is preached through them.

We don't have to develop a thorough sociological profile of North American adolescents to answer the question, "Who are kids?" We have the answer in hand. They are part of the body of Christ; the part that lives in the adolescent world, the part that will reach that world if it is to be reached. They are not yet mature, but they are mature enough to be who they are. Kids need not measure up to adult standards to be considered for the big time. The importance of their place in the family of God is implicit.

There. We've said it. Now, when we set our minds to understanding the subcultural characteristics of the kids' world, it will be to understand and establish rapport, to communicate and program more effectively. We need not establish credibility for kids, only to recognize it. Our task is not to confer a stripped-down adult integrity on them, but to acknowledge and respect the inherent integrity of the class and every individual.

> # When folks talk about Youth Sunday, I wonder, "Who is this for?"

Of one thing we are fairly sure: Youth Sunday is unlike anything else in a kid's world (the closest approximations are school performances—done largely for parents and squirming siblings). It's not that there's anything wrong with such exercises. They do, after

as a real estate executive is the ambassador for Jesus in her circle of influence, so the senior high kid is the advance man for the Kingdom of Heaven on his campus.

Kids are not useful to the Kingdom inasmuch as they wear wing tips and panty hose and

2. WHY DO WE WANT TO INVOLVE KIDS IN THE CHURCH?

———— ∎ ————

Perhaps this inquiry is more obvious than the one just finished. At the very least, it follows from the "Who are kids?" question.

Why does the good parent insist that each child take an active role in the family's life together? For the inconvenience of the offspring? To increase the work of cleaning up after Junior? Certainly not.

Kids participate in family living because that's what families are all about. Children are raised as a result of their interaction with the rest of the family.

Does a parent view his child rearing as preparation for the "next generation"? Not unless he's working on an epic novel. Chances are he is working on a successful family *right now.* Thoughts about the distant future are subordinated to the concerns of braces and Algebra II and coming home on time.

In the church, our nurture of kids has a similar character—or should have. Not that the future is unimportant, but that the future can only be reached through the present.

Kids don't need to learn what it means to walk the corridors of power in the church—how to govern, how to preach, usher, read Scripture, lead singing. Those lessons have their own seasons. Kids need to learn to live with Christ and to represent Him faithfully to their generation. Scripture makes much of the idea of generations; not with any apparent attempt at the isolation of age groups but to focus on what it means to walk with God for a lifetime. No one is too young to represent Christ to her generation. Note the encouragement of Paul to Timothy: "Don't let anyone look down on you because you are young, but set an example for the believers in speech, in life, in love, in faith and in purity" (I Timothy 4:12). You don't have to be a grown-up to pull your weight in the church.

> *Kids need to learn to live with Christ and to represent Him faithfully to their generation.*

Our obligation in getting kids into the life of the church is to prepare them for life in the world. That will surely focus on what it means to serve God's purpose in their own generation.

What we mean by *involvement,* then, is to include kids in the life of the church as *kids.* We want to nurture them, to enable them to be who God has called them to be right now and to help them do the things that flow from that identity. We will be wildly creative about the ways in which we help adolescents express their identification with Christ—knocking down subcultural barriers, speaking the Gospel in the language of the day. And we will resist mightily the temptation to put a sweater on the dog—to squeeze kids into roles that lack meaning because they lack points of reference in the adolescent world. In short, we will treat kids as if they are important to the church because they are part of it, tennis shoes and all.

Getting to It

———— ∎ ————

Following is a series of brief thoughts on getting kids involved in the church.

1. *Determine that youth ministry will take its place in the flow of the church's life.* Be aggressive about making youth ministry a point of entry into the church—not only for kids, but for whole families who will be attracted by our esteem for their youngsters. See the youth program as a part of the process that begins in childhood—or in adolescence when kids enter the church through the youth group—and continues for a lifetime.

2. *Think before you act.* Some programs ought to be discontinued, others never begun, because they violate the integrity of kids. It can be a tricky issue, especially in light of short-term losses sure to be chronicled by well-meaning folks who just want to see kids doing things around the church. Even so, ask "Why?" Then ask "What?"

3. *Build relationships with kids.* The most effective youth workers are men and women who know kids—not people who know about kids, people who know individual kids by name and by heart. The more adults you can persuade to get involved with kids, even for a couple of hours a week, the more success you'll have in getting kids involved in the life of the congregation. The process is so simple: "Hey, I'm going to church tonight. How about if I pick you up? We'll get a pizza on the way home." Make that offer enough times and you're bound to find kids willing to take you up on it. And if the invitation is to a ball game or

something else going on in the kids' world, watch out!

4. *Involve parents.* Be as open with parents as you can be. Tell them what's going on, what's in the future, how things went last month. Tell them over a cup of coffee, by telephone, in a photocopied letter, through the grapevine. And get parents involved in preparing their children for involvement in the church. Teach moms and dads how to ask questions and guide discussions about what's going on in worship, Christian education, outreach, missions, and fellowship. Form a parents' committee to advise and support you. Maybe they'll even work with you.

5. *Understand your community.* For better or worse, people choose churches, like most everything else, for what they can get out of them. Being sensitive to matters of taste and theology, give 'em what they want. Find an itch and scratch it. Look for hot spots in the school community and tackle them. Give attention to the relational problems that face kids: friendship, getting along at home, dating, breaking up, sexual ethics, divorce, peer pressure, and cliques. Talk about the physical and emotional changes they're going through. Persuade your pastor to talk about these things, or at least mention them from time to time. By paying attention to felt needs you'll gain the opportunity to deal with unfelt needs as well, to prepare kids for what's coming later.

6. *Stretch kids beyond their world.* Kids live in an age-group ghetto partly because it's comfortable. Take kids into situations that extend beyond their experience: a meeting of the church board, a retirement community, a hospital, a prison, a slum, a day-care center, a classical music concert (a rock concert), a big city (a farm), an ethnic ghetto. You get the point.

7. *Challenge kids to serve.* In strategies ranging from peer-group leadership to missions projects, help kids learn to serve. Service doesn't come naturally for most of us, but it is necessary to growth and involvement. Warning: Service is not the same as work. A car wash to raise money for the youth fund may be too self-serving to qualify as service. The servant is guaranteed no reward except from her master . . .

8. *Create a nurturing atmosphere.* Give kids permission to be kids. Expect them to act their age—neither older nor younger than they are. Let them discover that they are safe with you and they'll want to be with you.

9. *Teach kids to worship.* There are statistics which suggest that an adolescent who worships (only) is more likely to be in church ten years later than the kid who is in Sunday school (only). Why not both? Help kids understand the selfless act of worship—not for what they get out of it but for what they bring to it.

Reprise: What Is Involvement?

— ∎ —

When we see that God does what He wants to do, the clouds part and we get a glimpse of His glory. "Behold: I do a new thing!" God keeps creating congregations and youth groups that look and act and even "feel" different from any others.

"Involvement" is defined by what God is creating in your congregation, in your youth group. The only rule for defining involvement is the rule of integrity. If we ask "Why?" before we ask "What?" we'll seldom make really big mistakes. □

Jim Hancock is director of youth ministries at Solana Beach Presbyterian Church, Solana Beach, California. He contributes regularly to Youthworker *and* Group *and leads seminars at the National Youth Workers' Convention.*

Today's Church in Today's World

Frequent references have been made to a "youth culture" in which adolescents are segregated from the rest of society. That subculture is centered around educational structures that group students by age as opposed to, say, interest or achievement.

The interaction between kids and adults is almost exclusively related to task-oriented roles: student/educator, part-time employee/supervisor, athlete/coach, musician/teacher, consumer/supplier. In most cases, the adult is hired to interact with the adolescent and the value of the exchange is defined by the extent to which performance approaches an "adult" level. Beyond these typically formal relationships, there is little voluntary association.

The Church repeats these social relationships to near perfection. Because it is a voluntary organization, there is slightly more elective contact between adults and kids, but it is difficult to find ways in which the Church differs from the world in this regard.

—Jim Hancock

Ways to Involve Youth in the Church

Three senior pastors share their views.

1

I used to be a pastor in a large Baptist church. When I arrived, the youth group was totally separate from the church. Kids would go away to college, and because there was no more youth group, feel there was no more place for the church in their lives. So I worked to tie kids to the entire church.

I made sure there were no youth programs that stood on their own, apart from the larger church. For example, I never baptized any of the youth in separate "youth only" services, as the former youth pastor had done. We used no logos, no names for the youth group unless those identifiers were "whole church" oriented. I made sure that no one was a sponsor or worked with the youth who wasn't an active member of the church. Finally, I encouraged all officers of the youth group to regularly attend church services. As the leadership kids modeled that, the other kids came along.

In the church I pastor now, with only about 16 kids, involvement comes more naturally, because kids know adults outside of seeing them in church services.

Larry Osborne, *senior pastor, North Coast Evangelical Free Church, Oceanside, California*

2

There's no magic to involvement. Young people are looking for meaning in their lives, and the church can be an important source of meaning. The biggest problem is that usually the things we ask them to do are menial housekeeping chores you can't get adults to do. There are meaningful things that can be done–ministering in a nursing home, adopting a grandparent, visiting shut-ins— where kids, on a regular basis, keep in touch with people.

Kids have a number of things to say in terms of worship life, educational offerings, social ministry: they can get turned on to things the way they ought to be. That can be a very healthy thing for a congregation's life. It can be a way of revitalizing what adults are doing as they live out their ministry to the world.

The natural age differences and different interests of youth and adults tend to divide. I'm not sure that the differences are bad, as long as it never becomes "us against them." We can celebrate our differences. One way to do that is to have a youth group and a particular age group of adults work together on a project, or come together to talk about family life, morality, or music. It can begin a set of interchanges that can open new doors.

John R. Scarafia, Jr., *pastor of St. Timothy's Lutheran Church, Grand Island, New York*

3

Church programs are always looking for volunteers. Find some specific ways young people from your group can volunteer to be part of some programs, assist in some ministries, or aid in the mission of the church. Look for short-term commitments initially in order for your young people to get exposure. Perhaps have them look on it as an "experiment in infiltration." Have them approach the congregational structure as if they were alien agents seeking to infiltrate that local church for a "higher cause." Have them set a goal to befriend one new adult during the experiment in order to influence him or her to become a youth advocate. I suspect youth will be amazed at the opportunities and be able to overcome some of the feelings of helplessness that come from not being personally involved.

Dr. Gary W. Downing, *executive minister, Colonial Church, Edina, Minnesota*

Helping kids

cope with the

Great Church

Turn-off

Jogging shoes for feet of CLAY

On the outside this church had a lot going for it. It began in the ministry of prominent and gifted leaders. Among its members were some very talented, dedicated people. But the way it developed internally—in plain sight of its most sensitive and idealistic youth— was a tragedy and disgrace. Sex and money scandals, petty divisions, and self-centered people all made this congregation a spiritual eyesore. It had clay feet clear up to its armpits.

BY STEPHEN BOARD

This church should probably go unnamed since it developed into quite a scandal, but I'll identify it later.

Uncovered Flaws

———— ∎ ————

"I can't get our young people to accept that the Gospel changes lives when it has not changed the lives of some of our charter members," a youth leader was heard to say. Her husband added, "Our kids are pushed into taking sides in church fights and factions that they don't know anything about. The whole point of Christianity is obscured by these human representatives."

Anyone who works with youth or new Christians has a major problem like this. Young people haven't developed the knack of covering up the flaws of the church. They haven't learned to bracket out the scandal. Some of them even relish those warts on the face of high profession: "So, all those judgmental, nit-picking older folk have problems of their own! They don't get along with each other, they attack the pastor, and their marriages are shaky. Now they can get off my back!"

In short, when it comes to the visible church—the one most visible to your youth—"glorious things of thee" are *not* spoken. So what do you do next?

Honesty

———— ∎ ————

Let's at least be honest with our young people. A prominent theologian shocked his audience on one occasion by saying, "The church is like Noah's ark. You can only stand the stink on the inside because of the storm on the outside." We're talking about both a human and a divine institution. Everything human falls short of the

> ## Let's be honest with young people: The church is both a human and divine institution.

ideal, including government, families, and churches.

"You may like math but not your math teacher," I told a 13-year-old with exactly that problem. And I knew he liked popular music but did not admire all popular musicians. He liked tennis but not all famous tennis champions. To face the salt-and-pepper mix of the church may itself be the main growing experience a Christian young person needs. And facing it is inevitable.

Equally, they must be honest with us. Their complaints about the church may be a way of deflecting a hassle with their parents, who support the church. The church may be the lightning rod that's catching all the charged-up hostile atmosphere from a strict home or Christian school. Adult leaders can hardly be expected to pick up all that baggage and trudge along sympathetically beside such youth. But we can raise their sights.

Heady Doctrine

———— ∎ ————

Ask yourself, "How do I handle the hypocrisy, the failings, the disappointment in other Christians?"

Probably you will answer, "I have a separate vision that overcomes all that." That is, you have an understanding of who Christ is, what He is doing on the earth, what you think He wants you to do—and all that enables you to rise above the problems you see in any local setting.

No higher vantage point on the church can ever be reached than from the altitude of its Head, Christ Himself. This is what Paul urges on his readers in Ephesians when he says Christ is making the church "holy, cleansing her by the washing with water through the word." Not yet is the church "radiant," "without stain or wrinkle or any other blemish," nor is it yet, in even one instance, "holy and blameless." But that's where things are headed because of the Head of the church. The journey is already under way.

Some people think doctrine like this is too remote to be useful. But the Biblical writers made it useful, and we ought to be able to draw the connections as well. To put handles on that doctrine, however, we will need some practical experiences for the adolescent.

A basic starting point: How vivid is the Head of the Church to your teens? If they can strengthen a living friendship with Christ, the other problems will diminish in importance.

As youth begin to know who Christ is and what He has done, they will be able to serve the church, not just criticize it. After Paul's famous description of Christ in Colossians 1:15-20 ("He is before all things, and in him all things hold together"), he goes on to say, "I fill up in my flesh what is still lacking in regard to Christ's afflictions, for the sake of his body." First he understands Christ, then he can serve the people who name Christ.

This argues for some clear content about the Christian faith in our programming. No youth program will do its job if it is merely keeping the kids off the street. Nor can we be content with simply acquainting them with the church as an institution. We have a mission to introduce them to their Saviour and King who will change their lives.

Other Christians

Next, we can show young Christians a variety of redeemed humanity. Supposing you lived in Jerusalem in the first century. If you met one disciple and he was Judas, what would you think of the Christian cause? How about if you met only Judas and Peter? How about if you met only James and John, while they were trying to call down lightning on whole cities? Or Nicodemus while he was still a secret disciple?

Every additional Christian we meet fleshes out our picture of what the Church is like. In the Letter to the Philippians, Paul did not let two feuding members, Euodia and Syntyche (4:2), dominate the picture he had of this tiny church. He had seen others who paid a great personal price for their Christian commitment, like

> **We have a mission to introduce kids to their Savior and King who will change their lives.**

Timothy and Epaphroditus (2:25).

This may call for biographies of famous Christians. We are bound to have a bigger picture of Christian people after reading about Corrie ten Boom or Charles Colson. Some help will come through films and videos. You'll want to use guest speakers, camps, conferences, retreats, joint meetings, and trips out of town—all to acquaint your rather provincial young people with some relevant, dedicated examples to challenge their stereotypes of adult believers.

Jesus talked about disciples who were impatient with the visible "field" of God's people. They

wanted to pull up the weeds and just have wheat. He urged patience—wait for God to identify the weeds at the End. Adolescents are not known for patience. But their involvement will turn their attention to bigger issues and they will learn patience as a side effect.

Somewhere along the way, a growing Christian teen will get the picture: "Hey, I'm part of something bigger than I thought! The church is not just *them*; it's me, too." And when that insight breaks through, we need to be ready with ways for kids to invest in the church—to buy into it and consider themselves official stockholders. If we can harness their activism and let them build on to the church they know, whatever form that may take, the very activity will give them ownership in the total cause.

That scandalous church I mentioned at first was not the one in your community you may have been thinking of. It was the church at Corinth in A.D. 60 or so. You know: the one Paul said had its treasure in clay pots. Just like your church. Just like you. And me. □

Stephen Board is Vice-President and General Manager of Harold Shaw Publishers and former editor of Eternity *and His magazines. Steve has two teenage children.*

Small Church Suggestions

The #1 frustration in working with small churches is battling the attitude that small isn't okay. Small isn't necessarily bad.

Rejoice that small churches more naturally create a feeling of "family" and closeness. Combat the "small is less" mentality:

■ Emphasize *relational* ministry vs. *programmatic*. Programs that mandate large numbers support a "bigger is better" attitude.

■ Match young people with adults in the congregation. Encourage them to spend time together—talking, eating, going out for a Coke, joining in a common interest. Develop one-

on-one opportunities for faith sharing and prayer.

■ Spotlight individuals. Post kids' accomplishments in school and sports on your bulletin board.

■ Brainstorm places one carload of young people can go with an adult driver. Pick one place and go!

From Group *magazine, "Small Churches & Youth Ministry," by Joani Schultz, February, 1985.*

The Religious World of American Teenagers

Startling results of a Gallup study

"The shape of religion in America in the years ahead will be determined in considerable measure by the developing religious beliefs and practices of the nation's 25 million teenagers." So goes the intro to Gallup's study, *The Religious World of Teenagers.* Of the teens surveyed, 50 percent claimed to be Protestant, 38 percent Catholic, 3 percent Jewish, 3 percent gave other responses, and 6 percent claimed no religious preference. One teenager in every five would identify himself as "Evangelical."

Some survey highlights:
- 95 percent say they believe in God, and they are more likely to feel close to God than the average religiously inclined adult.
- Eight in ten say that religion plays a very important or fairly important role in their lives.
- Only 6 percent claim no religious preference and 70 percent claim church membership.

To the average teen, however, church attendance has little bearing on the quality of one's religion. Teenagers are critical of the church in these areas:
- The church, they say, is not reaching out to the people it should be serving.
- Teens have negative feelings toward churchgoers.
- Churches are not dealing with the basics of faith and are not appealing to youth on a deeper spiritual level, according to teens.
- Churches are deficient in providing an atmosphere of excitement and warmth.

Adapted by permission from CAMPUS LIFE Leader's Guide.

☐

Church Barriers to Teenagers

There are some parallels between the feelings of a teenager and a handicapped person when they come to a church activity. One way of becoming more aware of the barriers that exist in many churches for teenagers is to come with a physical disability to a church building. Have the teenagers come to church one Sunday on crutches, in wheelchairs, blindfolded, or with earplugs. While it is a game, it may help call attention to some of the physical ways we create a hostile environment to anyone who doesn't fit our conventional approach to Sunday morning activities. Have the young people explain they are doing an experiment in understanding the church's physical environment. But, have them gather afterward to talk about what happened and how they felt. Perhaps you could gather a few adult friends who were there informally to chat about how to make the church activities more open to people with different needs. In that context, you might have a chance to illustrate how young people have some specialized needs that should not cause them to be unintentionally excluded. Out of your experience and conversations a small group of youth advocates could emerge to help make some positive changes to help kids feel more accepted.

Dr. Gary W. Downing, executive minister, The Colonial Church, Edina, Minnesota

☐

Involving youth in the church begins with a solid youth ministry.

5 Tests For Successful MINISTRY

Let's go back to the basics. What is essential for effective youth ministry, whether you're working with church kids or unchurched kids, in a large or small church, as a lay person or full-time?

Consider these five tests.

Test #1—
Do You Give Students a Warm Welcome?

Dr. Glenn Heck from National College in Evanston, Illinois, has said, "You can do everything else wrong, but if you do two things right, you'll come out a winner." The first thing is, simply: Give students a warm welcome.

A few years ago, I attended an orientation for the Unification Church (the Moonies) in San Francisco. The one thing I remember about that meeting was how friendly, warm, and caring the people were to me. From the moment I walked into the room until I left, I had a guide explaining everything. Cults are growing because they have learned to give a warm welcome. In the same way, every effective youth ministry I have observed has an effective welcoming system.

Students enter your youth program with one question on their minds—"Will I fit in?" We need to provide welcoming guides to help them break into the group.

A guide may simply be a greeter at the door, or a wall with pictures about the program. There, kids who feel uncomfortable can read, stand around, and hopefully be picked up by another student. For the unchurched kid, a guide may

be a recent convert. For the apathetic church kid, the guide may be you building a relationship with him or her outside of church activities.

John was a disinterested high school student in my church. I asked John's parents if he had any special interests and found out he was very interested in repairing old model railroad cars. My parents had recently cleaned out their attic and sent me my old train set. So I picked up John from school one day and we spent the next three hours in my basement, unwrapping car after car. John explained to me the details of each car. During the course of that conversation, we talked about God, family, and his relationship with the church. After a year or so, John became a leader in our youth group. I asked him why he was disinterested at first

BY RIDGE BURNS

and how he became interested. He said he became interested the day we spent looking at the train.

Test #2—
Do You Have Adults Who Are Crazy About Students?

Heck's second can't-miss suggestion is this: Give students an adult who's crazy about them.

In our group, 70 percent of our students are involved in small group Bible studies called Core Groups. The leader of each Core Group contacts his or her students on a weekly basis. Core Group leaders also spend time where the students are—football games, badminton matches, and debates.

Meg, a student in our group, wasgoing to a big formal event at her school. Another leader and I asked her to get ready early so we could see how she looked. Because adult leaders in the group are crazy about Meg, she works hard to make the youth group alive. A warm welcome brings in students from outside; an encouraging adult keeps them coming back.

Test #3—
Do You Have Students Working with You?

Every youth group event at Wheaton Bible Church is coordinated by a team of students. Those students plan, direct, and usually allocate the funds for each event. Those students have a lot of ownership in each event, so they generate a lot of interest in the activity among their peers.

In my office, there are photographs of every mission trip youth have taken since I have been at Wheaton Bible Church—photographs representing 13 trips

and 26 work sites. Each one of those work sites was directed by a student leader. When students come into my office and look at those photographs, they identify the trips, not by the adult leadership, but by the student who was in charge. They say, "That was Sue's trip to Mendenhall, Mississippi," or "That was J.T.'s trip to Mexico."

I'm a believer that the best way to minister to students is through students. Do you have a group of students who communicate the goals, purposes, and programs of the youth ministry to their peers?

Test #4—
Are You on Track?

In Tom Peters's and Robert Waterman's book, *In Search of Excellence,* one of the eight attributes that emerged as a prerequisite for success in the corporate world was the principle of sticking with the things you know best. The book says, "While there are few exceptions, the odds for excellent performance seem to strongly favor those companies who stay reasonably close to the business that they know." Youth workers need to stay close to the business they know: youth ministry.

A youth worker can often get sidetracked into being many things: camp director, coach, counselor, teacher, media technician, and on and on. But the fundamentals of youth ministry are simple. Are you ministering to students, and are they growing?

Recently we ran an outreach event. Its sole purpose was to lead students to Jesus Christ. Shortly before the event, some students and I got together to pray. One of the students prayed that other students would come to know Jesus Christ as Savior. I thought to

myself, "In the last two weeks of planning this event, I forgot this was our purpose."

Are you sidetracked? Maybe you need to return to the basics.

Test #5—
Are You Prepared for Ministry?

As I look around my office, I see diplomas, awards, shelves of books including commentaries, how-to manuals for youth ministry, devotionals, and books for small groups. But none of those have fully prepared me for the daily requirements of ministry. The only thing that makes me actively sensitive and involved with the students is the leading of the Spirit, and that comes through a quiet time with God. The way to be prepared is to get your heart set.

The first time I went to Mexico with a group, we prepared all the right flannelgraphs, stories, and crafts. But we were not prepared for the little orphan kids who wanted only to sit on our laps and be loved. The way to prepare for that ministry was to prepare the program, and the heart.

You are a role model for kids' spiritual growth. You need a quiet time with God. You need wisdom to handle situations that confront you. You need to be a guide led by the Spirit of God.

Consider your youth ministry in light of these five tests. If you can answer yes to all five, you are on the way to an effective ministry. □

Ridge Burns *is pastor to high school students at Wheaton Bible Church, Wheaton, Illinois. A graduate of Trinity Evangelical Divinity School, Deerfield, Illinois, Ridge has also served churches near San Francisco and Detroit.*

Aim

Overview

You'll Need

1-7-90

Why the Church?

To help teens understand that the Church—past, present, and future—is a divine institution given and guided by God. Key passages: Acts 2:1-4, 42-47; 4:33; 6:1-7; I Thessalonians 4:13-18.

The last two thousand years of history record the rise and fall of many human organizations. Meanwhile the Church has spread to every major civilization on Planet Earth! God didn't just establish the Church and then desert it. Kids need to understand that God guides and works through the Church even today. And God has promised a glorious future for His Bride.

1. How's Church? (Checklist) 10 min.
   □ How-You-Feel-About-the-Church Checklist (activity piece A1 from the back of this book)
   □ pencils

2. Old-Time Religion (Bible/history lesson) 20-25 min.
   □ paper
   □ pencils
   □ Bibles
   □ The Church in Motion (activity piece A2)

3. That's Not All (Bible discussion) 10-15 min.
   □ Bibles

4. So Why Attend? (Wrap-up) 5-10 min.

BY DAN RUNYON

*E*xamining and discussing feelings about church. **Some of you probably have strong feelings about church. Others may not care one way or the other about church. Here's your chance to express your feelings.**

Hand out copies of the "How-You-Feel-About-the-Church Checklist" (activity piece A1 from the back of this book). Let kids go over the sheet, checking how they feel about the statements there. Then discuss what they have to say. Try not to make any judgments yourself. If a kid makes a very negative statement, you could ask other kids if they agree with it. Let kids air their feelings, then move on to the following:

Churches do have problems. But problems arise because the people in churches are imperfect. We're going to take a look at why the Church is still around after all these years in spite of its troubles. And we're going to see just what makes the Church so important.

---

*S*eeing how God designed the Church and how He keeps acting through it. Help kids think about how God designed and guides the Church through this exercise.

Suppose you have just invented a new computer. It is easy to use, cheap, and plays great games. Everybody wants one! You're getting orders faster than you can fill them. So you decide to start a new business with yourself as president. What will you call your business?

Let kids quickly come up with a name.

You need to mass-produce your computer. This means hiring a production manager who will be responsible for putting out a quality product—and fast! Your reputation depends on his or her success, so choose well. List three characteristics you would look for in the person you hire:

Take suggestions from kids.

Now list five more things you have to do if you want your business to make and sell 100,000 computers within the next 12 months.

Take suggestions from kids.

These are just a few of the hassles you would face as president of a new business. Think what a challenge it would be to organize the Church! There are millions upon millions of "customers" who speak hundreds of different languages in all corners of the globe. Think of some of the brilliant administrative moves God made so

1. How's Church?

(Checklist) 10 min.

2. Old-Time Religion

(Bible/history lesson) 20-25 min.

3. That's Not All

(Bible discussion)
10-15 min.

the Church would run well. Let's take a look at how He got it started.

Have your kids read Acts 2:1-4; 42-47; 4:33.

■ **How did the Church get started? Who was responsible for it?**

■ **What do these verses tell us about the purpose of the Church?**

■ **What made the Church grow?**

Divide your kids into groups of four or five. Explain that now you are going to look at how the Church grew after its beginning. Pass out copies of "The Church in Motion," activity piece A2. Have each group read over the list and add other things God has done in His Church since the early days. Have the groups report their additions.

■ **How can you prove that God didn't stop working in His Church after those first days?**

■ **How can you prove that God is still at work in His Church today?**

Discussing how God is going to work in the future of the Church.
We've seen that God has worked in His Church since its beginning and right up to the present. But do we know what He's going to do in the future? The Bible tells us much of what is still in store for God's Church.

Have kids read I Thessalonians 4:13-18. Ask for a volunteer to tell in his or her own words what Paul is describing here.

Before your meeting, write each of the following questions on a separate slip of paper. Fold each paper; mix them in a paper bag. Have kids draw one question at a time and answer it, with the help of the rest of the group.

■ **Is the event Paul describes something you look forward to? Why or why not?**

■ **Who will be involved?**

■ **What should we do since we know what is going to happen? How can we do that?**

■ **What do you think God wants the Church to be like in 50 years if Christ has not yet returned? (You will be in your 60s.)**

■ **How should a Christian's attitude toward the future be different than a non-Christian's attitude?**

■ **What problems could happen if Christians concentrate on the return of Christ and ignore things right now?**

■ **What problems could happen if Christians concentrate on things right now and ignore the return of Christ?**

---

*L*ooking at what makes church worth attending. Have your kids look back at the checklist they completed at the beginning of the meeting. Have them note how any of their feelings about the Church may have changed through this meeting. Ask for volunteers to share what they may have learned. Then ask these questions:

■ **So what does all this mean to us? How should this affect the way we look at the Church?**

■ **What would you tell someone who said, "I don't get anything out of my church. I can be a better Christian reading and praying on my own"?**

Let kids think about this one for a while. If they don't start giving good reasons, question them about some of the reasons that can be derived from this meeting: God is working through the Church; God will take care of His own; A glorious future awaits the Church; etc.

Try having kids pray to end the meeting, thanking God for starting the Church and continuing to work in and through it.

Dan Runyon earned his M.A. in communications from Wheaton Graduate School, Wheaton, Illinois. Formerly a college professor and an editor, Dan is now a full-time free-lance writer.

4. So Why Attend?

(Wrap-up) 5-10 min.

Aim

Overview

You'll Need

1-14-90

Treasure in Human Vessels

To help kids see that the church has problems because it is made up of humans. But God works in and through it in spite of problems. Key passage: II Corinthians 4:7.

The church is a divine institution with Christ as its Head. Yet everyone who participates in it is human. This means that mistakes, hypocrisy, failure, and problems are inevitable. In spite of problems, the church is a success whenever it recognizes that the "all-surpassing power is from God and not from us" (II Corinthians 4:7).

1. Only Human (Simulation) 15-20 min.
   □ Church Meeting (activity piece B1 from the back of this book)

2. Smooth Machine (Human machine) 10-15 min.
   □ slips of paper
   □ hat or paper bag

3. Monkey Wrench? (Work sheet) 15-20 min.
   □ Working Part or Monkey Wrench? (activity piece B2)
   □ Bibles
   □ pencils

4. Follow the Head (prayer) 5 min.

5. Optional: Body Without a Brain (Obstacle course)
   □ paper sack or blindfolds

BY DAN RUNYON

Simulating a church board meeting to realize that the Church has problems because it's composed of humans. Ask for five volunteers for the simulation, "Church Meeting." Instructions and character role cards are found on activity piece B1 in the back of this book. Distribute one role card to each volunteer. Quietly read the instructions to the volunteers and give them a few minutes to study their characters. Then introduce the simulation to the group by reading aloud the "situation" section and introducing the characters listed below.

CHARACTERS

1) Gloria Swanson, an elderly widow. She's been with the church since it started. 2) Tanya Jackson, church treasurer. 3) David Bird, youth pastor. 4) Steven McConnel, a businessman and leader in the church. 5) Lance Burkhart, close friend of Pastor Thompson. They are about the same age; so are their children.

Allow the volunteers seven to ten minutes of good interaction before halting the simulation for discussion.

■ **How common are problems like these in churches in general? In our church?**

■ **What do church problems like these prove?**

■ **What is God's attitude toward church problems like the one in the simulation?**

■ **Why doesn't God just destroy the Church for such stupidity?**

Since the Church is made up of humans, problems are inevitable. But God, in His grace, uses the Church in spite of its problems.

1. Only Human

(Simulation) 15-20 min.

Illustrating the way God wants churches to run by making human machines. Before the meeting, write the names of various household appliances and machines on slips of paper and place them in a hat or paper bag. You will need one slip for every group of four or five kids. You may want to use machines like: a lawn mower, blow dryer, electric mixer, coffeepot, stereo, can opener, or typewriter.

Divide kids into groups and have each one draw a slip of paper. Give each group a few minutes to study its machine. Then have the groups take turns making their machines (complete with sound effects) while the other groups try to guess what they're making.

■ **What makes these machines run smoothly?**

(Each part does its job and they cooperate or work together.)

2. Smooth Machine

(Human machine) 10-15 min.

■ **How are churches like these machines?**

■ **What are some things in churches that disrupt their smooth operation?**

(Gossip, fighting over the color of the carpet, pride, selfishness, unfriendliness, etc.)

■ **How does God help churches run smoothly?**

(He teaches us through the Bible; He gives us pastors and leaders to guide us; He gives us the Holy Spirit to make us more Christlike.)

---

3. Monkey Wrench?

(Work sheet) 15-20 min.

Examining our own attitudes in our church.
Throughout history, the Church has grown and prospered in the face of many problems. Yet, many of the problems in our local churches could be avoided if we would behave as the Scriptures instruct us. Except in the face of clearly dangerous teachings or threats, there should be harmony and cooperation in each church.

Have you ever thought that maybe *you* are the source of some of the problems in our church? Let's find out if we are working parts or monkey wrenches in the works.

Pass out the work sheet "Working Part or Monkey Wrench?" (activity piece B2). Each kid will need one copy and a pencil. Kids should work individually.

During the last five minutes of this section have the kids find a partner. (If there is an extra kid you be the partner.) Without sharing what concrete action they plan to take, have partners commit themselves to check on each other at least once before the next meeting to make sure they're following the plan.

---

4. Follow The Head

(Prayer) 5 min.

Recognizing Christ as the Head of the Church and seeking His help and guidance.
Our task as individuals in the Church is not an easy one, but as Colossians 1: 18a says of Christ: "And he is the head of the body, the church." As our Head, Christ not only points us in the right direction, but also gives us the strength to go in that direction.

With kids still paired off, have the partners take turns praying for one another that each would follow the Headship of Christ.

Allow them a few minutes to pray, then close the meeting by thanking God for His guidance and asking Him to make you attentive followers.

5. Optional: Body Without A Brain

(Obstacle course)

Note: If you have extra time, you might try the additional activity below.

P laying a game to demonstrate the importance of keeping Christ as the Head of the Church. Clear as large a space as possible. Have half of the students form a human obstacle course in this space. Have the other half walk through it one at a time. First allow them to look at the obstacles. Then put paper sacks over their heads (or some other form of blindfold). Finally, spin the blindfolded kids a few times and have them traverse the course. After they have finished, let the groups switch activities. Be careful that no one gets hurt.

■ **What is the hardest part about walking around blindfolded?**
■ **Do churches ever walk "blindfolded"? In what way?**
(When they stop following God's guidance and revelation.)
■ **What are some mistakes that churches might make by walking "blindfolded"?**
(Getting away from Biblical truth; not fulfilling the purpose that God has given them; becoming poor witnesses because of so much sin within.)
■ **What is the worst mistake a church can make?**
(Trying to function without Christ as its Head.)

Dan Runyon *earned his M.A. in communications from Wheaton Graduate School, Wheaton, Illinois. Formerly a college professor and an editor, Dan is now a full-time free-lance writer.*

Aim

Overview

You'll Need

Peer Pressure In the Church

To help kids realize that there is great help in standing together—but they must stand on the right ground. Key passage: Ecclesiastes 4:9, 10, 12.

Peer pressure is as real in churches as anywhere else. That pressure can be a source of encouragement, or it can lead to destructive things like cliquishness and the inability to make individual decisions. This meeting will help students become aware of the potential and the dangers of pressures within the youth group, and will encourage them to help each other instead of dragging each other down.

1. Gilda Y. Groupie (Discussion sheet) 10-15 min.
   □ Gilda Y. Groupie (activity piece C1 from the back of this book)
   □ pencils

2. Baal Pressure (Bible study and letter writing) 20-25 min.
   □ Bibles
   □ paper and pencils

3. Positive Pressure (Matching answers/discussion) 10-15 min.
   □ Pressure Inventory (activity piece C2)
   □ Bibles

4. Releasing the Pressure (Application and prayer) 5 min.
   □ Bibles

BY BILL REIF

*R*ecognizing the possible dangers and benefits of youth group pressure. Pass out pencils and copies of "Gilda Y. Groupie," activity piece C1 from the back of this book. Quickly point out and describe the different aspects of Gilda's uniform and attitude.

■ **How would you like to be in a church with a whole youth group of Gildas? Why or why not?**

Have your kids think silently about the next two questions.

■ **Do you ever feel pressure here to be something that you're not, just to fit in or be accepted?**

■ **If you wanted to be in the "in crowd" here, would you have to become something that you're not?"**

Ask the kids to write down any pressure they feel at the bottom of the picture. Assure them that they won't be forced to share what they write. If several kids don't write anything, you might humorously point out that peer pressure is at work, keeping them from writing anything.

Obviously, peer pressure exists, even here at our church. It can be harmful, but it could potentially be a force for good—helping us to become the people we really want to be. Let's look at how we can make our relationships here into friendships that help.

---

*S*eeing the positive and negative impact of group peer pressure.

Religious peer pressure was operating even in the Old Testament. The story of Elijah and the prophets of Baal illustrates both the good and the bad impacts of that pressure.

Have kids form groups of four to six. Try to put at least one talkative kid in each group. Write the following references on a chalkboard: I Kings 18:22-39; 19:14-18. Have all your kids read both passages. Then have half the groups write letters (one per group) as if they were Elijah, writing to a friend about the pressures he felt at the beginning of the event and then at the end. Have the other groups write as if they were one of the prophets of Baal writing to a friend. After about ten minutes have the groups quickly share and discuss their letters.

If kids don't suggest it, point out that things would probably be easier for Elijah now that he knew he wasn't alone. A prophet of Baal, on the other hand, would have been much better off without his "religious" friends. The pressure they provided led to negative results.

Many times, having an encouraging friend around

1. Gilda Y. Groupie

(Discussion sheet)
10-15 min.

2. Baal Pressure

(Bible study and letter writing)
20-25 min.

makes all the difference when we face a pressure-packed situation.

Read Daniel 3:16-25 to the entire group.

■ **What kind of religious pressure did these three friends provide for each other?**

■ **How do you think they would have responded if only one of them had been there?**

■ **Who was the fourth person who showed up in the furnace?**

Many commentators believe this was a pre-incarnate appearance of Jesus Himself. Help kids see that this is the difference between positive and negative religious peer pressure: not just that you have church friends to do stuff with, but that you have friends who want to include Jesus in all that they do.

---

3. Positive Pressure

(Matching answers/ discussion) 10-15 min.

*D*iscovering ways to become positive influences on each other.

If Jesus is at the center of our relationships, then we should influence each other for the good. We should be positive encouragement to each other, not a drag or discouragement.

Pick a large guy to represent a *bad influence*. Then pick a smaller guy to represent *Joe Youthgroup* trying to stand alone against the *bad influence*. Have the big guy try to carry *Joe* across the room while *Joe* resists (set limits on how physical they can be). Once the *bad influence* has accomplished his task, have him leave the room. Then let *Joe* pick any two friends to help him. Give them 30 seconds to come up with a plan, then let the *bad influence* back in the room and give him the same instructions as the first time. If the *bad influence* still appears to be winning, call in more reinforcements.

(Note: Be sure to choose people who aren't sensitive about being big or small. A way to bypass this potential problem is to ask someone to tear in half one or two pages from a phone book. Then have the person try to tear 50 or 100 pages. Use the object lesson to make the same point of "strength in numbers.")

After a short struggle, call a halt to the hostilities and read Ecclesiastes 4:9, 10, 12. Point out that it's obvious that we need each other to stand against certain influences. Whether it's as a help in standing firm or as a catalyst to a fall, we *do* influence each other.

Pass out the "Pressure Inventory," activity piece C2, and quickly read through the instructions. Answer any questions, then let kids begin. When they're finished, discuss kids' answers, pointing out again that we will always influence each other, either positively or negatively. Here are the correct answers: 1-A, 2-H, 3-I, 4-C, 5-E, 6-L, 7-J, 8-D, 9-G, 10-B, 11-F, 12-K.

Ask kids to point out any items on the sheet that they feel the group is already pretty good at, and have them give some examples of that positive influence in action. You might need to make some observations of your own here to prime the discussion.

Then ask kids to discuss any areas that still need work. Do not ask for examples, but ask them to come up with some ways they might go from being negative to being positive influencers. Again, have some ideas of your own already in mind to help them along.

*C*onsidering how to change from negative to positive influencers and trusting God to make that difference.
Read Hebrews 10:24, 25.

■ **What does it mean to "consider how"?**

Considering means taking time to think something completely through. This means we should take time to consider our impact on people in our church and how we might encourage them.

■ **What are some things that you might need to "consider" doing about improving your influence in this group?**

Give kids a minute to think about this question and encourage them to write down any specific thoughts. Be prepared to share an example out of your own life if time allows.

Conclude the meeting by pointing out the faithfulness of God in making us more and more like Jesus every day. Encourage kids to take action on what they have seen in this meeting. Close with prayer, asking God to continue to be faithful in opening our eyes to where we need change, and to make those changes in us.

Bill Reif *is a veteran youth minister and speaker from Dothan, Alabama. Bill speaks at many camps and conferences each year, in addition to Youth Specialties' regional seminars and National Youth Workers' Convention.*

□

4. Releasing The Pressure

(Application and prayer) 5 min.

Aim

Overview

You'll Need

Support
Your Local Church

To guide teens in discovering the special qualities of their church. Key passage: Ephesians 4:15, 16.

Any kid with friends quickly discovers that all families are not alike: In their friends' families, the parents are different, the rules are different, the free-time activities are different. So it goes with churches. One meets in a huge cathedral, another in a storefront. In one, ministers wear fancy robes; in another, jeans. And those are only the surface differences. Many kids wonder: "Why is Tina's church so different from mine? Which one's right?" This meeting helps kids understand the various ways their local church is different from other churches, and appreciate the special qualities each church brings to the worldwide Church.

1. The Perfect Church (Advertisements) 15-20 min.

   ☐ poster board (one per group)
   ☐ markers
   ☐ magazines, scissors, tape
   ☐ optional: construction paper (various colors)

2. Seven Ordinary Churches (Bible study) 10-15 min.

   ☐ Seven Ordinary Churches (activity piece D1 from the back of this book)
   ☐ Bibles
   ☐ pencils

3. My Church (Evaluation) 20-25 min.

   ☐ chalkboard and chalk, or newsprint
   ☐ church bulletins, newsletters, annual reports

BY KENT LINDBERG

1. The Perfect Church

(Skits) 15-20 min.

Advertising the "perfect" church. All of us would like to attend the "perfect" church. For youth workers, the perfect church would have no financial problems, an abundance of volunteers, and a limitless supply of resources for youth ministry. This activity helps kids think about the perfect church for them.

Divide kids into groups of three. (One way to do this is to hand each kid a slip of colored paper—be sure there are three slips of each color. Ask them to find others with the same color.)

Ask each group to pretend that it could start from scratch and create the perfect church. Each group will set the guidelines and special qualities of its perfect church—jeans and sneakers are worn on Sunday mornings, services are held at Disney World, whatever. Then it will advertise the special qualities it comes up with on an advertising poster.

Distribute poster board, scissors, magazines, tape, and markers to each group. Encourage kids to be imaginative as they create posters advertising their perfect churches.

When groups are finished, have each one present its poster, explaining the special qualities of its church, and why those qualities make it perfect. For fun, have kids look over the various posters and vote for the "most perfect" one. Then talk about it:

■ **How were these perfect churches alike?**

■ **How were they different?**

■ **What made the "most perfect," perfect?**

Emphasize the various differences that emerge. Point out that people disagree about what would make a perfect church. Some people like one thing; some another. If you want to strengthen this idea in kids' minds, have them think about what a ten-year-old would consider is a perfect church, as opposed to what an 80-year-old would consider the perfect church.

Tie together the activity:

Did you ever wonder why churches are so different? We've just seen why. Churches are different because the people in them are different.

Think about your family. It is not exactly like any other family in the entire world, because your mom, your dad, and you are not like anybody else in the entire world.

And just as every family is special in its own way, every church is special in its own way. Tonight, we're going to look at some of the things that make our own church different from other churches—and special.

2. Seven Ordinary Churches

(Bible study) 10-15 min.

*S*tudying Scripture to see that even churches during New Testament times were different from each other, with their own strengths and weaknesses. ■ **Why do you think no church can ever really be "perfect"?**

(Aside from the fact that humans are sinful and create problems, any group of people larger than about two could never agree on what made the perfect church.)

■ **What would you say to someone who thought our church was right and every other Christian church was wrong?**

As kids throw this one around, you might again refer to the idea that churches are like families. Families aren't *right* or *wrong,* they just are. Sure, some families are weaker than others, some are even falling apart. But each family has its own strengths, weaknesses, and special qualities to work with.

Sometimes people get the idea that churches during New Testament times were perfect. But each church, even then, was very different. Each one had its own strengths and weaknesses.

Divide kids into groups (groups from the first activity are fine). Pass out pencils, Bibles, and a copy of the "Seven Ordinary Churches" Bible study sheet (activity piece D1 from the back of this book) to each group.

Have each group study the Bible references listed to discover one strength and weakness of each church. If you're short on time, assign just a few of the churches to each group.

Have groups report their answers. The important point to bring out is that each church had its own special strengths and weaknesses. The same is true today: No church is perfect, but each is special in its own way.

3. My Church

(Evaluation) 20-25 minutes

*T*hinking through the special qualities of our own church. On a chalkboard or piece of newsprint, list the phrase *Special Qualities of Our Church.* Have kids brainstorm characteristics of your church which help to set it apart from other churches they know about. You might suggest these categories:

■ Number of people. ■ Ages of people. ■ Type of building. ■ Type of community. ■ Size of youth group. ■ Special programs. ■ Style of worship. ■ Special things we believe. ■ Who makes church decisions and how. ■ Some of our biggest strengths as a church. ■ Some of our biggest weaknesses as a church.

Meeting D

Have a volunteer scribe list the ideas contributed. Encourage kids to be honest, yet constructive, without naming or cutting down individuals. For example, kids may suggest strengths such as "youth group is fun" and "pastors are nice" and weaknesses such as "worship services not very interesting" or "sermons too long."

To help stir kids' thinking, you might make available the church bulletin, newsletter, or annual reports. If you can get similar materials from neighboring churches, kids will be able to see the unique qualities of their own church.

(For a different approach, invite the senior pastor and/or other congregational leaders to the meeting. Have them discuss questions such as: "In what ways is our church different from other churches in the area?" "What do you think are the major strengths of this church? Major weaknesses?" "How can the youth group contribute more to this church?")

Have kids look over (think about) the various qualities that were named. Which are they most excited about? Which would they like to change? Which can the youth group have a direct impact upon?

■ **Suppose a kid from our church was frustrated with our church, and wanted to stop coming or go to another church. How might you encourage him or her to stay?**

(Sure, our church has weaknesses, but it also has some real strengths; No church is perfect; Stay and try to make it better.)

Close with prayer thanking God for some of your church's strengths.

Kent Lindberg *is associate pastor of Centerville Community Church, Centerville, Ohio. He is a graduate of Trinity Evangelical Divinity School, Deerfield, Illinois.*

Aim

Overview

You'll Need

Body Language

To encourage kids that there is a place for them in your church and to help them discover it. Key passage: I Corinthians 12:12-27.

Teens often view themselves as outsiders, even while they are within a church. They need to understand their importance as part of the Body of Christ. This session will help kids discover that God views their gifts and abilities as essential contributions to the church. This session will also assist teens in developing a more positive self-image.

1. Team Drawing (Team project) 15-20 min.
   □ pencils and paper
   □ Team Assignments (activity piece E1 from the back of this book)
   □ Team Drawing (activity piece E2)
   □ optional: blindfolds, prizes

2. Gift Catalog (Magazine or hymnbook search) 10-15 min.
   □ magazines or hymnbooks
   □ chalkboard and chalk, or newsprint and markers

3. Gift Exchange (Brainstorming) 15-20 min.
   □ pencils and small slips of paper

4. Into Action (Prayer) 5 min.
   □ Bibles

BY KENT LINDBERG

1. Team Drawing

(Team project) 15-20 min.

Participating in a team project to see that the church needs many different people working together. Form groups of four (or three, if necessary). Explain that each group's goal is to draw a copy of a picture. But first, before anyone sees the picture, each person in the group needs to be assigned his or her job.

Distribute a copy of the "Team Assignments" (activity piece E1 from the back of this book) to each group. Each group should decide which of its members will handle each of the assignments listed. (If you have three people in a group, omit the "FEET" and allow the "HANDS" to hold the paper as he or she draws.)

When everyone knows his or her assignment, distribute a piece of paper and pencil to the "HANDS" in each group, and a copy of the "Team Drawing" (activity piece E2 from the back of this book) to the "EYES" in each group. Be sure that no one else sees the drawing. The best way to do this is to blindfold everyone on the team except the "EYES." A simpler way is to have the EYES person sit behind the others with his or her back to the others.

Give kids seven minutes to complete their copy of the drawing. Call time and have groups display their drawings. Choose the best drawing and award the winning group a prize such as fast-food coupons.

- **How did you feel about your final drawing?**
- **What frustrated you most?**

(The frustrations will vary depending on which assignment kids had. The Eyes, for example, were probably frustrated to see a drawing develop that was different from what they were describing.)

- **Which person was most important to the success of the drawing? Why? Which was least important? Why?**

(There may be some rationale for rating the hands more important than the feet, but kids will probably point out that everyone was essential.)

- **Sum up the main thing someone could learn from being part of one of these teams.**

In order to complete the drawing, everyone was necessary. The same thing applies in this youth group and in our church: Everyone is needed. Everyone is important. But there's a problem: Sometimes we don't feel needed or important.

- **Why do you think sometimes kids don't feel needed by the youth group and church?**

Give kids plenty of time to think this over. Two key ideas: 1) We don't think we have much to offer. We don't sing,

2. Gift Catalog

(Magazine or hymn-book search) 10-15 min.

and we aren't very good at leading, etc., so we feel left out. 2) We know we have a lot to offer, but we feel that other people won't give us a chance to offer it. For example, someone might be a talented artist, but nobody gives him or her the chance to create something.

First, we're going to see what each of us can offer to the youth group and to the church. We all have important things to offer, and we need to discover them. Second, we're going to look at ways to use our gifts in this group and church.

*D*etermining our God-given talents and abilities. Ask kids to take turns reading I Corinthians 12:12-27. Point out that Paul shatters the concept of who counts. Each person's importance is not built on looks or wealth, or how noticeable they are, but the fact that each is loved and gifted by God. Even those who view themselves as blob believers are special and important.

Make available a variety of magazines and have each person tear out words or pictures relating to talents and abilities he or she has been given by God. Or pass out hymnbooks, and have kids identify hymn phrases that describe their gift areas. Whichever method you choose, help kids think by listing the following general categories on a chalkboard or piece of newsprint. They paint in broad strokes the many gifts from God listed in Scripture.

- HELPING PEOPLE, LISTENING

- ART, MUSIC, EXPRESSING FEELINGS

- TEACHING, LEADING, MOTIVATING, PERSUADING

- SPORTS, ACTIVE HANDS-ON WORK

- FAITH, PRAYER, MIRACLES

- MAKING MONEY, GIVING

- READING, WRITING, COMMUNICATING

- SOLVING PROBLEMS, COMING UP WITH IDEAS

- SPEAKING, ACTING

While kids flip through the magazines or hymnbooks, circulate and help ones who may have trouble believing they have positive qualities and abilities. Loosen up kids by explaining that you only want a general idea of areas they

Meeting E

believe God has blessed them in. Their knowledge and use of God's gifts will grow and change throughout their lives.

*T*hinking of specific ways to use our gifts in the youth group and/or church. Have kids form groups of three or four (the groups from the first activity are fine). In the small groups, each person should explain the magazine pictures or hymn phrases he or she chose. The group should then brainstorm specific ways that person could use his or her gifts in the youth group and/or church. Let's say Sheila tore out magazine pictures showing her abilities in sports (especially swimming) and listening to people. The group might suggest: Start a summer swim program (maybe part of VBS) for kids in the church; invite kids from swim team to youth group; pray for the people who confide in her.

Encourage kids to think creatively, even wildly, and to come up with as many ideas as they can for each person. So the ideas don't get lost, have kids write them on small slips of paper.

*P*raying about specific ways to use our gifts as members of the Body of Christ. Have each kid silently choose one of the ideas on his or her slip of paper, or another way to contribute to the youth group or church. If kids are open with each other, have them share what they want to work on with others in the small groups.

Close your meeting by having kids pray for one another in the small groups.

Kent Lindberg *is associate pastor of Centerville Community Church, Centerville, Ohio. He is a graduate of Trinity Evangelical Divinity School, Deerfield, Illinois.*

3. Gift Exchange

(Brainstorming)
15-20 min.

4. Into Action

(Prayer) 5 min.

More Bright Ideas

1
Lone Crane

Have kids stand apart so they can't touch anyone or anything. They should each grab one foot and stand like a crane with eyes closed. The one who remains standing this way the longest is the winner. A kid is out if he opens his eyes, drops his foot, or falls. Then repeat the activity, with one change: Kids may help support each other. The moral is: No one can stand for long as a lone-crane Christian. We need each other for support, and we need the light of God's Word to see where we stand.

2
Love Feast

Have kids plan and serve a potluck supper after church one Sunday. Make it an appreciation/fellowship dinner for your church. The program could include testimonies from kids about what God is doing in their lives and what they appreciate about your church. Or, it could be reminiscences of adults about how they first became involved in your church.

3
Trivial Pursuit

Collect a variety of trivia about your church from members old and young. Then set up a road rally with a series of questions based on the trivia you've collected. With each question comes a clue to where the answer can be found. First car back to the meeting place with all questions answered is the winner.

BY ANNE DINNAN

4
Pray Together

"Spur one another on to love and good works." Establish prayer partners for a specified period of time. Each pair (best to keep them same sex) is responsible to meet together at least once a week outside of church to share concerns with one another and pray together. This is a great way to build fellowship in your group, but it will take some encouragement on your part. Usually, the idea of praying with someone—really praying—is threatening. But once you overcome that barrier, it will be the most powerful feature of your group. To break the ice, perhaps you could pray with kids individually.

5
Sponsor Program

Develop a sponsor program to build relationships between kids and adults in your church. Shoot for a low ratio of adults to kids: one to one, or one to two. Send a letter to adults in your church asking them to befriend one youth in the church for a specific time commitment, say, one year. Suggest activities they can do with their youth together to break the ice.

6
Saints Party

Plan a costume party for All Saints' Day (or any day) to celebrate great Christians from church history. (In New Testament terminology all who profess the name of Christ are *saints,* whether they are special in other ways or not. So anyone is fair game for this.) Break your group up into pairs (or threes) and assign each set a period of church history from the first century to the present. Give kids a couple of weeks to research their period of history and decide which saints they want to dress as. See if there are books in your own library, pastor's library, or public library for information.

Assign some kids to help plan games and refreshments. The main fun at the party will come when kids show up in their costumes and try to explain who they are. You might also play a "Who Am I?" guessing game if their choices are familiar.

By the way, this works especially well as an intergenerational activity. Let your kids plan it for the whole church—have games, and refreshments; each family or Sunday school class should do its own research.

Illustration by Donna Nelson

7
Battle Rest

"The battle is the Lord's," and we are His foot soldiers. On forced marches, soldiers would get very tired. Often, when·they stopped to rest, they literally sat on one another. You try it! Form a close circle, with everyone looking at the back of the person in front of him or her. Have everyone sit on the knees of the person behind. Thus, you can "bear one another's burdens." While in this position, talk about how the Church is a community where we come together to rest and be refreshed.

More Bright Ideas

8
Acts Of Mercy

"I have come not to be served, but to serve." Introduce your kids to the ministry of the church in acts of mercy. Take them on pastoral calls to the elderly, sick, and shut-in. Let them do something concrete to help, like taking a shut-in her groceries, or transporting a poor young mother to the laundromat. Take kids on calls to the hospitalized and let them read Scripture. This is the nuts and bolts of ministry. Let your kids in early on the *grace* of giving.

9
World Christians

Many young people (and adults as well) have a very provincial view of the Church. They know what their church is like, but few have any kind of a view of the Church universal. Help them break out of that mind-set by having a World Christian Festival.

Set up interest centers on various countries with food, artifacts, and information about the Church in that place. Plan a multilingual worship service with your main theme—"The Kingdom of God: Every Kindred, Tribe, and Nation." Sing songs or read familiar Scriptures in other languages. It would be particularly effective if you had a guest from another country to speak about the church in his or her land.

For information in planning this event, check with your church or denominational missions program. Other sources:
- *World Christian* magazine (Pasadena, CA)
- *Breakthrough* magazine (Slavic Gospel Association, Wheaton, IL)

As a follow-up to this event, how about establishing rapport with the youth of a church in another country.

10
Underground Church

Find a place outdoors or in the basement or attic of a kid's home to hold a secret fellowship and prayer service. In every age, Christians somewhere have been persecuted for their faith—either by other Christians who thought differently, or by a hostile government. Help give kids an appreciation of such suffering by holding this clandestine meeting.

To simulate conditions in many repressive countries, sing hymns and share Scripture from memory only, since there are often few hymnals and Bibles available in many of these countries. Make the emphasis at your meeting prayer for those still suffering persecution for their faith in today's world.

11
Youth Survey

Take a survey of how kids in your youth group are currently involved at church, and how they'd like to be. Based on the survey, help kids move beyond ushering and helping in the nursery to fresh ideas for your church: a youth visitation team, drama or clown troupe, whatever lets kids thrive in the Church as kids.

12
Film Festival

Films are an entertaining and thought-provoking way to introduce kids to church history. So get the popcorn out and enjoy these at a lock-in, retreat, or series of evening meetings. Just a few of the films you might show:

■ *Martin Luther* (Lutheran Church Productions), a 1953 classic.

■ *John Wycliffe: The Morning Star* (Gateway Films, Lansdale, Pa.).

■ *A Man for All Seasons* about Sir Thomas More, Henry VIII, and the English Reformation. This classic secular film is available from most libraries. (You may find only the edited version, *A Matter of Conscience: Henry VIII & Sir Thomas More.*)

Serve refreshments and discuss the issues raised in each film, such as the authority of Scripture, freedom of religion, persecution and prejudice, etc. Suggest further reading.

Additional resource: Check out the new quarterly magazine, *Christian History,* published by Christian History Institute of Worcester, Pa. (subscription address: P.O. Box 3000, Dept. C, Denville, NJ 07834).

13
Your Church

Search the archives for old pictures and documents about your church. Interview old-timers. When was the church founded? What were the original facilities like? What were the church's distinctions? What was it known for in the community? Who were the leading founders? Who was the first pastor? What missionaries were sent out from your church? What charities or foundations were started or supported by your church? What were youth organizations like years ago? Publish your research in your church's newsletter.

14
Sing To Me

It's hardly a new idea, but it is often a neglected one. Have a hymn sing, "singspiration," "songfest," whatever you want to call it. Scripture tells us that one of the evidences of the activity of the Holy Spirit in the Church is that we sing! If your kids are intimidated by singing, one of your goals should be to get them relaxed and open enough to sing. Bring in someone who plays guitar or piano, sit in comfortable chairs or on a carpeted floor, dim the lights, and have a night of singing and sharing.

15
On the Board

Do a simulation of a typical church board meeting. This will give kids a good idea of how human the church really is, but also give them an insight into the complexities of church life, and how God works through it all. Be careful not to model your roleplay too closely to your own situation; be general. Establish some roles for kids to play: pastor, denomination official (if appropriate), elder, deacon, trustee, etc. Some characters could be innovative types, others more traditional. (See Activity #1 in the meeting, "Treasure in Human Vessels," or Marlene LeFever's excellent book, *Creative Teaching Methods* [Cook], for ways to set this up.) Prepare a typical agenda. Some situations to be dealt with could include: What to do with some money that's been donated: make needed repairs to facilities, pay outstanding bills, give it to a family in need, use it for the camping ministry, etc. Kids will have to establish priorities and make tough decisions. Other situations to discuss might be: ways to reach out to the community or dealing with a troublesome member.

16
Adore Him

"And God placed all things under his feet and appointed him to be head over everything for the church, which is his body, the fullness of him who fills everything in every way."

Jesus is what it's all about! We are *His* Church, *His* body. Spend an evening focusing in on who Jesus is, adoring Him. Read Scriptures that talk about Christ's redeeming work and His supremacy and power (Ephesians, Colossians, or Revelation). Then, if appropriate, celebrate that feast that Christ commanded His Church to keep—that feast that draws us together (even if we understand it differently), cleanses us, and renews our faith.

18
Many Members

Visit churches in your community from other denominations and ethnic backgrounds. What are the similarities, differences? Are they major or minor? Discuss the fellowship you can have in Christ with those whose traditions are different. But emphasize what sets your denomination apart doctrinally or historically from others.

Get together with the youth group from one of these churches, especially one whose members are of a different ethnic background. (If you are a well-integrated church, congratulations! It's been said that the most segregated time in America is 11:00 to 12:00 on Sunday morning.) Just playing sports together and sharing food will bring your kids together and promote understanding. Afterwards, study Ephesians 2:11-22.

17
Make a Machine

Divide your group into trios or quartets and give them five minutes to build a human machine to demonstrate how church members must work together—each using his or her unique gifts. Some machines to try might be: a vending machine, a toaster, a lawn mower, a can opener, whatever! (For additional ideas, see Activity #2 in the meeting, "Treasure in Human Vessels.")

19
Future Church

Books like *Future Shock* and *Megatrends* talk about all the changes we have seen and can expect to see in the future. Society is becoming more and more complex. How will this affect the Church?

For fun, have kids create posters advertising what they think the typical church will be like in 100 years. After kids present their posters, discuss:

■ What challenges will the Church face?

■ How will technology affect it? Changes in family structure? In governments?

■ What does Matthew 16:18b tell you about the future of the Church?

Anne Dinnan is editor of youth publications for David C. Cook Publishing Co. She has contributed to the award-winning Young Teen Action *series (Cook), and works with teenagers each week at her church in Elgin, Illinois.*

Stages of Group Development

Building a close church group depends on understanding how your group will change

BY GARY W. DOWNING

I was baffled. Our small group had started so positively. Everybody came and everyone seemed to do whatever was suggested with enthusiasm. But by the third or fourth meeting, the glow began to dim. Some members were still very positive, but others started to complain about little, unimportant details. After a couple more weeks, some of the original people started to skip meetings. They all had plausible excuses, but something was missing. I didn't know what to do. I began to wonder if I was doing something to drive people away. It was so exciting when we began, but now it just wasn't much fun.

Have you had that experience in a group? Whether you were a leader or a participant, have you noticed how often groups start "high," then level off? Group experts have discovered natural *stages*, or phases, through which all groups pass. While some of the levels are identified differently by different experts, the general flow remains the same. By anticipating and encouraging these changes, you can help a group grow qualitatively towards in-depth relationships.

The Honeymoon Stage

First, there is the honeymoon stage of a group. For whatever reason (including just starting a new season) a group forms, and there is a surge of acceptance and enthusiasm. There is a positive attitude and a superficial acceptance of others in the group. This is a fun stage, a time of new energy and receptivity. It generates the kind of feeling that teachers and students may feel the first week of class or a coach and players may experience at first. It's the stage that keeps us coming back for more. However, too many groups in our society are satisfied with this superficial level of relationships. It demands very little and creates an illusion of commitment among the members.

The Neutral Stage

The neutral stage sets in when people in the group are disappointed to discover that Heaven has not yet arrived on earth. There are real people with real problems in the group. The functions of the group are beginning to conflict with other activities. Members begin to voice their concerns. They begin to offer different ideas about the way the group should operate to meet their needs. Teenagers often express boredom (verbally or nonverbally). They begin to question the programs, activities, and content discussed by the group. While there may be no overt challenges to leadership, there will be less loyalty. People begin to wear thin on each other; some drop away.

The Watershed

This is the watershed point for most groups. Members either fade away through apathy or confront the need to reconsider why they want to be together as a group. Phase three is a time of anxiety for the participants. If they haven't gone off to find their ideal in another group, they will have to face realistically what is happening and decide whether to pay the price of commitment to continue.

I had been part of a monthly fellowship group for several years. We didn't know each other when we started, but our first impressions were positive. It took several meetings before the initial enthusiasm began to wear off. (The time between meetings is less important than the amount of time together.) The first sign of trouble came when we began to find it increasingly difficult to schedule time to meet. We began to complain to our spouses about other members in the group. When we were together we were all smiles, but our commitment was very superficial. It took the honesty of one member finally to call us to consider where we were going (or not going) as a group.

It was painful to admit none of us were as committed to the group as we acted. When Eric blew the whistle we all felt guilty, but also felt relieved. It was not until that point we could begin to understand each other and accept each other in spite of weaknesses and problems.

The Acceptance Stage

Acceptance, the fourth phase, was crucial for our group to begin to experience some unity and common mission. While few groups ever "arrive," deeper relationships that result from conflict make it usually worth the effort. When a group constructively handles problems, an energy is created that is greater than the sum of the energy each individual brings to the group.

That is one way of describing the "Body life" that can occur when Christ is the center and source of your group. If He has called you together, then He will provide the energy and vision it takes to experience the loving relationships God intends for all of us together.

Nurturing Activities

1. You can help a group develop by identifying why the members have gathered. Some phrases that can be shared:
- I'm here because . . .
- One thing that would make this group a positive experience for me . . .
- I think the purpose for our group should be . . .
- One word I would like to be able to use to describe our group in a month is . . .
- My best experience in a previous group was . . .

Have participants share in groups of three or four. Collect responses (without judgment) on a chalkboard. Identify common themes. Work toward consensus on a purpose for the group. With a clear purpose understood by everyone, a group will develop more rapidly in a way that is affirming and exciting to the participants.

2. Establish ground rules for behavior in the group. You may even want to negotiate written norms. Some examples:

(a) *If we want to be "together," we have to be together.* Personal participation is the key to building a cohesive group. Maybe you need to develop a minimal "contract" for attendance, including how long members are committed to the group.

(b) *We need to pay respect to receive respect.* Some practical ways to pay respect include rules like:
1) Don't interrupt—listen before you talk.
2) Don't probe—give people space.
3) Don't give advice—let people ask for it.
4) Don't judge—leave that to God.

(c) *What goes around, comes around.* What is shared here stays in the group. Trust is crucial to depth in our group. We want to create a safe and sacred space to grow.

□

Dr. Gary W. Downing *is executive minister of the Colonial Church of Edina, Minnesota. Formerly he was executive director for Youth Leadership and was part of the National Training Staff for Young Life.*

BY ANNIE AND STEVE WAMBERG

As the Church Turns

A HUMOROUS SKETCH

Characters

Fallen Angel: Wears trench coat, carries clipboard and pencil. Should have fedora with horns attached. Arrogant, proud.

Good Angel: Wears baseball jacket, glove and cap with halo wired to it. Easygoing.

Mrs. McGillicuddy: Woman in church. Easy to play her as a snob, but try not to.

Pastor Middleman: You might want to model this character after your own pastor.

Jason: Typical young guy.

Teens 1, 2, 3: Typical kids. (Note: Lines can be divided to accommodate more teens.)

Pastor Jeff: Youth pastor.

Gladys: Lady in the church.

Florence: Another lady in the church.

Ruth: Middle-aged woman who dresses young, carrying a backpack. Lots of energy!

Props

- ☐ two stepladders of equal height
- ☐ two game clickers ("crickets") if Angels can't snap fingers loudly enough to be heard
- ☐ clipboard and pencil
- ☐ folding chairs (two for Pastor Middleman, one for each member of the congregation)
- ☐ lectern or podium on wheels
- ☐ papers to represent church constitution
- ☐ backpack
- ☐ loaves of bread wrapped in foil
- ☐ offstage piano or recording playing "The Church's One Foundation"

As the Church Turns

As scenes shift, characters involved should move their chairs to face the audience, then back to a side view as their spot finishes.

As the play opens, congregation (everyone but PASTOR MIDDLEMAN, MRS. McGILLICUDDY, and the ANGELS) is seated with chairs facing pulpit. The FALLEN ANGEL is on a ladder off to side. The GOOD ANGEL has not yet entered, but he, too, will sit on a ladder looking down on congregation. With the exception of the opening dialogue, all dialogue between the people is started, and most of it is stopped, by the ANGELS snapping their fingers (shown in the script as "click!").

MRS. McGILLICUDDY: Now need I remind you, dear Pastor, that it was *my* generous gift that made it possible for the church to purchase that lovely organ?

PASTOR: Well, no . . . but . . .

FALLEN ANGEL: Click! (*cuts off PASTOR'S line and sings, "Isn't she lovely?"*) I had to start out with one of my best tricks—convincing people that the church could not function without them! Old Mrs. McGillicuddy over there thinks she owns the music program because she gave most of the money for the new organ. And we all know how much a pipe organ costs! Listen . . .

(*GOOD ANGEL should enter and climb up his ladder during MRS. McGILICUDDY'S next line.*)

MRS. McGILLICUDDY: Well, Pastor, you know I never want to be pushy . . .

GOOD ANGEL: Click! Let's get a few things straight, here!

FALLEN ANGEL: Hey! You're horning in on my show!

GOOD ANGEL: I think I have a little more right to be in church than you do!

FALLEN ANGEL: Oh. *(pause)* I was just showing these folks *(points to the audience)* some of my better accomplishments.

GOOD ANGEL: That's cool *(slams hand into ball glove)*. But let's show them *both* sides. Click!

MRS. McGILLICUDDY *(to PASTOR)*: There're some folks down the road from us that need this *(slips or tosses him a wad of money)*. I'd rather it came from the church than me.

FALLEN ANGEL *(pretending he's playing a violin)*: Aw, you're breaking my heart. Click!

(JASON rises from his chair, goes to pulpit, and begins to push it slowly across the stage.)

PASTOR: Stop! *(panicked)* What are you doing?

JASON: I'm setting up for our wedding rehearsal.

PASTOR: But you're moving the pulpit furniture!

JASON: That's true. See, we wanted to have the . . .

PASTOR: Don't you know I could be fired if you move that?

JASON *(laughs)*: That's a good one!

PASTOR: No, I'm serious. Look! *(pulls paper out of pocket and points to it)* It's right in the church constitution that I can be fired without notice if the altar furniture is moved!

JASON: Come on! Nobody here would do that. We don't worship the furniture!

FALLEN ANGEL: Click! See? These humans are crazy! That one wasn't even my idea. *(to himself)* Although, I wish I'd thought of it—that's one *devil* of an idea!

GOOD ANGEL *(flabbergasted)*: You stopped him! You stopped him before he was done talking! No fair! Click!

PASTOR: See, it's right here *(points to paper)*. *(JASON shakes his head as he reads.)* This was done years ago. I guess they were just trying to protect the furniture. Probably after all the work it took to raise the funds to buy good furniture they didn't want some new preacher—or anyone for that matter—to ruin it.

JASON: Yeah, but to *fire* you!

PASTOR *(throws up his hands)*: Gotta go by the book! Let's see if we can't think of a new way to arrange your wedding party. . . . *(PASTOR puts his arm around JASON as they walk back to chairs.)*

FALLEN ANGEL: All right! All right! But here's one that's worked for 2,000 years! *(giggles with evil glee)* Go get 'em, kiddos! Click!

TEEN ONE: *(TEENS and PASTOR JEFF stand.)* I don't care what you say, Pastor Jeff, that old music stinks!

TEEN TWO: Yeah! Besides that, we did what you said. We went to the board and asked their permission to do something different in Sunday morning worship.

TEEN ONE: Yeah. And they just laughed at us when we said we wanted to do interpretive breakdancing!

TEEN THREE: The old stick-in-the-muds never like our ideas! They won't let anything change.

FALLEN ANGEL: Click! There, see? Two thousand years and they still keep the kids on the outskirts and won't allow change.

GOOD ANGEL: As usual, you're only letting these folks see half of the story. "And now, the rest of the story!" Click!

PASTOR JEFF: Even though you think they're old fogies, they really do help us out a lot. Mrs. Peters . . .

ONE *(cuts him off)*: *She* laughed the loudest at our worship ideas!

PASTOR JEFF *(chuckles)*: Yeah . . . well, she was the one who set up the camp scholarship fund.

ONE: Really?

PASTOR JEFF: Yup. And I know you're all *thrilled* with Mr. Sherman *(moans from the TEENS)*, but he's the one who suggested matching the funds to establish a college scholarship program.

THREE: You're kidding!

PASTOR JEFF: Not at all. The board wants you all to go as far as you can—but also wants to help find you a place to plug in now. They asked me if they could come to the next youth meeting since you came to theirs, to discuss ways for you all to feel a part.

TWO: You mean they're really coming to talk to us? At our meeting?

PASTOR JEFF: Really.

ONE, TWO & THREE: Maybe we can talk them into interpretive breakdancing! Yeah! We can demonstrate! Good Answer! Good Answer!

FALLEN ANGEL: Click! Oh, gross! Why did you make me watch that? I think I'm going to be sick . . .

GOOD ANGEL: You have my permission to leave.

FALLEN ANGEL: You're not getting rid of me that easily. Click!

(GLADYS, FLORENCE and RUTH stand up. GLADYS and FLORENCE are next to each other, RUTH is alone.)

GLADYS: I can't believe it!

FLORENCE: Hmmm?

GLADYS: Just look at Ruth! Look at what she's wearing! You'd think she was 14!

FLORENCE: Or trying to be. And carrying a backpack! She looks like she's heading for Girl Scout camp! Ha! Ha! Ha!

FALLEN ANGEL: Click! There you are. The adults can't even get along! And that's one problem that will never be solved *(laughs and looks self-satisfied)*.

GOOD ANGEL: Maybe. But do you ever watch till the end?

FALLEN ANGEL: I try to avoid endings. They can be so messy.

GOOD ANGEL: Right. Well, watch this. Click!

FLORENCE: Don't look now, but here she comes!

RUTH *(coming over to the ladies)*: Hello, girls!

FLORENCE, GLADYS *(nodding)*: Hi.

RUTH *(talking fast)*: I'm glad I caught you together! I was baking yesterday and, well, you know how zucchini is. A little goes a long way! And I thought, "Now, Ruth, who would enjoy this bread the most?" And right away you two came to my mind. *(FLORENCE and GLADYS glance at each other sheepishly.)* So here you are! Enjoy! *(RUTH hands them the foil-wrapped bread, and trots back to her seat.)*

GLADYS: Wasn't that sweet?

FLORENCE: Yes, but I still think she looks like a Girl Scout.

FALLEN ANGEL: Click! Ha! Now there's a perfect ending for you!

GOOD ANGEL: Well, I never said they were perfect. Not yet, anyway!

FALLEN ANGEL: That's for sure! And what about the family who has run the church for generations? Or the "we've-never-done-it-that-way-before" attitude? Backbiting! Infighting! Generations at odds! Power plays! Apathy! I tell you, it's all gonna fall around them. The whole structure is about to collapse! You see, God forgot to take out the weak links—people!

Ha ha ha! And that one slipup is going to cost Him His church! Ha!

GOOD ANGEL: You've been trying to tell me that for 2,000 years. Wake up and smell the brimstone! Haven't you read the end of the Book yet?

FALLEN ANGEL: Uh, well, I just can't seem to get through it.

GOOD ANGEL: You try to tell me that God made a mistake by leaving people in the Church—but when will you see what's really going on? I mean, it may take longer 'cause of all the monkey wrenches you're throwing in, but God gets things done through these people. Maybe it's just 'cause He started out right. *(Music up and under rest of dialogue softly: "The Church's One Foundation")* And by the way, I suggest you skip over and read the end of the Book. It's hot stuff! *(FALLEN ANGEL cringes)*
(PASTOR motions to congregation to stand, and all recite, in unison)

ALL: (Compiled from I Peter 2:4, 5; Eph. 2:20-22; I Cor. 12:27; Eph. 4:4-7, 12, 16) Come to Him, to that living stone, rejected by men but in God's sight chosen and precious; and like living stones be yourselves built into a spiritual house, with Christ Jesus himself as the chief cornerstone. In him the whole building is joined together and rises to become a holy temple in the Lord. And in him you, too, are being built together to become a dwelling in which God lives by his Spirit.

PASTOR & PASTOR JEFF: Now here is what I am trying to say: All of you together are the one body of Christ, and each one of you is a separate and necessary part of it.

ALL: We are all parts of one body, we have the same Spirit, and we have all been called to the same glorious future.

FLORENCE, GLADYS, RUTH *(putting arms around each other)*: For us there is only one Lord, one faith, one baptism . . .

TEENS: And we all have the same God and Father who is over us all . . .

JASON & MRS. McGILLICUDDY: And in us all . . .

ANY REMAINING: And living through every part of us. However, Christ has given each of us special abilities so that the body of Christ may be built up to a position of maturity, until we lovingly follow the truth at all times— . . .

GLADYS, FLORENCE, RUTH: Speaking truly . . .

MRS. McGILLICUDDY, PASTOR, JEFF: Dealing truly . . .

ALL TEENS: Living truly . . .

ALL: And so to become more and more in every way like Christ who is the head of His body, the church. Under His direction the whole body is fitted together perfectly, and each part in its own special way helps the other parts, so that the whole body is healthy and growing and full of love.

(During the last few lines the FALLEN ANGEL should become very disturbed and "slink" off stage. GOOD ANGEL should look very pleased with what is being said, nodding in approval, getting more and more excited as it goes on, until he finally bursts out with)

GOOD ANGEL: Amen! Amen!

ALL: Amen!

CURTAIN

□

Steve and Annie Wamberg *are the founders of Harvesthome Productions, an evangelistic arts and research organization. They perform concerts of original music, comedy, drama, and puppetry. They are also contributors to the award-winning* Young Teen Action *series (Cook).*

© 1986 David C. Cook Publishing Co. Permission granted to reproduce for ministry use only—not for resale.

Finding My Place in God's Family

Photo by Jim Whitmer

L O C K - I N   P L A N

Breakaway

Aim

BY PAUL BOOSTROM

To help kids realize each member's important contribution to the youth group.

Overview

Christianity teaches the remarkable understanding that all Christians belong to Jesus and therefore belong to each other. This isn't just flowery language, but a description of reality. Each of us can say: "I am part of the Body of Christ, and therefore I am important!"

In sharing this with a youth group, the problem is that a few kids think they are the only ones the youth group needs. Most kids, however, are sure they are the kind no one needs. So a key objective for this lock-in is that youth know the "stuff" vital to being special and needed is not human stuff, but divine. Everyone with the Spirit alive in him or her is special and needed by other Christians.

The lock-in reinforces these principles and thoughts:

Principles:
1. God makes us new.
2. God makes us unique.
3. God makes us for a purpose.

Thoughts:
1. I am important to the group.
2. Others need me.
3. I need to do my part.

You'll Need

- □ record player, Christian records
- □ Bibles
- □ volleyball and net
- □ small slips of paper, pencils
- □ optional: ingredients for making pizza
- □ chalkboard and chalk or newsprint and markers
- □ masking tape, transparent tape
- □ flashlights for each person
- □ paper plates
- □ cotton balls
- □ toothpicks
- □ long pieces of rope
- □ awards for Olympics
- □ enough copies of all BR activity pieces for all the participants

SCHEDULE

SCHEDULE

Finding My Place in God's Family

Evening

- Arrival and opening activity
- Orientation, Bible study #1: I Cor. 12
- "Do without" supper
- Bonus volleyball
- Snacks
- Study #2: Rom. 12 and Gal. 5
- Body life variety show
- Vespers: circles
- Lights out and stargazers

Morning

- Morning devotions and breakfast
- Study #3: Ex. 3 and 4
- Olympics and awards ceremony
- Closing

Evening Events

Arrival, Opening Activity

Play a favorite game that is active but not exhausting. This ensures that latecomers will miss a game rather than the first study.

Or, play records by very different Christian artists such as Amy Grant, Petra, and Mike Warnke. Later in the lock-in mention how these Christians, all very different, serve the Lord.

Orientation and Bible Study #1: I Cor. 12

Explain the theme and goals of the lock-in right away. Have one person read I Corinthians 12:1, 4-11. Note especially verses 7 and 11: The Holy Spirit gives gifts as He thinks best, not as we wish. He gives gifts to each person so that every Christian might benefit the rest of the Church.

Have other people take turns reading I Corinthians 12:12-26. Have one or two kids or adults (let them know ahead of time) share briefly an experience of feeling part of the Body of Christ, or of envying someone else's gift and discovering they also were of worth in the Body.

Then hand out copies of the "Me and the Body" sheets (activity piece BR1 from the back of this book) for each person to complete individually and then share with a partner.

"Do Without" Supper

A "do without" supper is not a matter of doing without food, but doing without one of our normal body members. Write one of the following body parts on a piece of paper: arms, legs, eyes, ears, nose; continue until you have one piece of paper for each person.

Before dinner, have each person draw one of the slips. Explain that each person has to eat dinner without the use of the body part listed. Provide

blindfolds, cotton or earplugs, rope to tie arms behind backs, and so on. The legless ones must be aided to the table, the armless ones must be fed by others, etc.

Alternative Supper: Let the kids make supper. Supply all the ingredients to make a pizza, but give each person only one item. (Large groups can be broken into table groupings.) Example: one person gets flour, another sauce, another cheese, another half of a recipe card, another the other half of the recipe card. Each person must contribute what he or she has in order for the group to eat.

Bonus Volleyball

Regular volleyball can be played by a team of ten, from which only three good players get to hit the ball. Bonus volleyball makes everyone important. The ball may be hit on one side as many times as a team wishes, within a 30-second time limit. For each

Breakaway

different player who hits the ball, the team can score a point (with one rule: one player may not hit the ball twice in a row). Example: If the ball is hit only by Robert and then the other team misses it, his team gets one point. But if it is hit by Robert, Mary, Tom, Robert again, Nancy, and Bill, the team gets five points for the five different people who touched it. Like regular volleyball, the point(s) are scored only if the other team fails to return the ball. Keep track of the 30-second limit and the number of team members who hit the ball on each play.

Snacks

Have some snacks during a cooling-off period between activities. Allow a little extra time if your group seems to need free time. Alternative: Serve snacks "do without" style, like supper. Have kids take different roles from the ones they had at supper.

Study #2: Rom. 12 and Gal. 5

Have one person read aloud Romans 12:3-8 and another read Galatians 5:22-26. Clarify the idea of gift as something given by another, and the idea of fruit as a natural growth. Follow discussion with the "I Am Survey" (activity piece BR2). Distribute copies for kids to discuss in pairs, or write the survey on a chalkboard and discuss it as a group.

■ What would our group be like if everyone were a leader? A follower? A loner?

Have each person think about the two people on either side, and why each person's qualities are important to the group. Have kids share their insights.

Body Life Variety Show

Have kids plan skits about the theme: "Finding My Place Within God's Family." The skits could be anything from 30-second commercials to one-act plays. Suggest a few examples to get kids going, then give them time to plan and practice. Groups that finish early can have free time until all the groups are ready.

Then have kids perform their skits in "The Body Life Variety Show." Encourage them to display lots of appreciation for each other.

Vespers

End the night officially with a vesper service. Pick songs appropriate to the lock-in, such as "We Are One in the Spirit." Capsulize the teaching from the evening, and/or add these thoughts on circles.

Let's sit in a circle. Hold hands. This is a circle, and we all belong to it. If (name of someone there) and (name of another person there) leave the circle (have them do so), we are less for their leaving. It's possible to have a small circle. (Choose three people to stand and hold hands.) Or smaller circle. (Have two kids stand and hold hands.) But you cannot be a circle by yourself. (Hold own hands extended in circle.) Stupid looking, isn't

it? We have a oneness in Jesus Christ and we need each other. Leaving the fellowship or leaving others out doesn't change that fact. We are one, and the Almighty God planned it that way.

Close with a prayer of thanksgiving and Communion, if appropriate for your group. Dismiss to prepare for bed. Announce Stargazers for all who are interested in staying up for a serious time of reflection.

Lights Out and Stargazers

Have adults stay in the sleeping quarters with those who choose not to participate in Stargazers.

Prepare for Stargazers by having a good reader make a tape of the script (activity piece BR3). If you are not able to have someone tape the speech, read it yourself. Have youth lie outside and watch the stars, or gaze out a window at unobstructed sky. Silence must be maintained, and everyone should sit apart from each other. After the tape is played, have kids return to their beds, still meditating silently.

Morning Events

━━━ ■ ━━━

Devotions and Breakfast

Start with an exercise song. Have someone lead in a little stretching. Then have a kid or adult share for two to three minutes about belonging. Sing a song, then follow with a closing prayer—also the table prayer for breakfast.

Study #3: Ex. 3 and 4

Choose three people to read the parts of Narrator, the Lord, and Moses in Exodus 3:1-7, 10-12 and 4:1-4, 6-7, 10-13.

Notice your average believer in God. Here he is, seeing a miracle, getting to know God personally, hearing the Lord's future plans for His life, and being promised power over his enemies. What does he do? He chickens out! He wants God to bless his life but let someone else do the hard stuff. He has excuses galore for not doing his part. But he is part of the people of God; he is called to do his important part.

■ How are you like Moses? What excuses might you give if God called you to do a hard job like that?

■ How are you not like Moses?

What has to be answered now, by the group and each one of us, is the important question, 'So what?' So what if God has made me new in Christ? So what if I am forgiven and important? So what if I am a member of the family of God and the church right here? What will that mean in my life and this group?

Allow time for answers. Recall I Corinthians 12:7. We have the Spirit to make us not only special but useful to the church and thus to the furthering of the Kingdom.

The answers you have given here have been great. But the answers each one of us lives after this lock-in are the real answers.

Olympics

This game time builds on the "body" theme of the retreat because it allows nonathletes to compete on teams with athletes. Form teams of about six people each by drawing names at random. Give each team a list of events (only the Olympic name). After every team has chosen its members for each event, explain and run the events.

Discus: use paper plates; farthest throw wins.

Shot put: use cotton balls; farthest throw wins.

Javelin: use toothpicks; farthest throw wins.

Marathon: guide an ant once around table; fastest ant wins.

4 X 400 relay: "crab walk" 15-25 feet and back; fastest team wins.

Joke: tell joke within two-min. limit; judges pick three funniest.

Tall tale: tell story within two-min. limit; judges pick funniest, craziest.

100-meter dash: entire team stands close together, is tied around with rope, then "mob walks" 25 feet and back; fastest team wins.

Vault: teams leapfrog 25 feet and back; fastest team wins.

Platform dive: dive in pool; judges pick biggest splash, silliest.

Give 300 points for first place, 200 for second, and 100 for third in each event. Total scores, and be creative with awards.

Closing

Stand in a circle to emphasize the teaching of the retreat. Have a few volunteers or everyone offer short prayers. □

Paul Boostrom *is pastor of First Christian Church in Janesville, Wisconsin. He has written two activity books for junior high youth groups,* The Hostage Game, *and* That's Tough *(both David C. Cook Publishing Co.).*

HOW-YOU-FEEL-ABOUT-THE-CHURCH

CHECKLIST

Check how you feel about each of the statements below.

		Strongly Agree	Agree	Neutral	Disagree	Strongly Disagree
1.	I enjoy attending church.	☐	☐	☐	☐	☐
2.	All churches have problems.	☐	☐	☐	☐	☐
3.	People created the Church to help them worship God.	☐	☐	☐	☐	☐
4.	Church is okay, but it doesn't mean much to me.	☐	☐	☐	☐	☐
5.	God loves and guides the Church.	☐	☐	☐	☐	☐
6.	Going to church is really more for people my parents' age.	☐	☐	☐	☐	☐
7.	There are a lot of hypocrites in church.	☐	☐	☐	☐	☐
8.	God can't work much through churches because of all their members' problems.	☐	☐	☐	☐	☐
9.	Anyone can benefit from attending church.	☐	☐	☐	☐	☐
10.	Attending church is mostly a waste of time.	☐	☐	☐	☐	☐
11.	I can serve God just as well without going to church.	☐	☐	☐	☐	☐
12.	Churches usually have good reasons for their policies.	☐	☐	☐	☐	☐

ACTIVITY PIECE A1 by Paul Woods © 1986 David C. Cook Publishing Co. Permission granted to reproduce for ministry use only—not for resale.

The Church in Motion!

An overview of some major events in Church history

AD 30
PENTECOST (Acts 2): The Christian Church begins with God's sending of the Holy Spirit.

64
NERO'S PERSECUTION: Persecution gets tough as Nero blames Christians for burning Rome. Many are fed to wild animals or burned alive. Today's score: Lions 7, Christians 0.

313
CHRISTIAN EMPEROR: After Christians have been persecuted for almost 300 years, the emperor, Constantine, becomes a Christian. Christianity becomes a legal religion of the Roman Empire. Nero turns over in his grave.

800
CHARLEMAGNE CROWNED: The king of the Franks is made emperor by the Pope. Promotes a dynamic new method of evangelism: Kill anyone who refuses to convert.

1095-1291
THE CRUSADES: Born of religious zeal, the Crusades are an attempt to rescue the Holy Land from the Muslims. The Christians lose, 5 to 3.

1517
THE REFORMATION: Martin Luther nails his complaints to a church door, leaving holes in the door and splitting the Church. Unable to accept unbiblical practices in the Catholic Church, Luther, Calvin, and Zwingli start the Protestant Church. Other Catholics, such as Teresa of Avila, try to combat the corruption from within.

1735
THE GREAT AWAKENING: Jonathan Edwards leads the awakening in America, preaching about a personal faith. John Wesley finds Christ in 1738 and becomes a leader of the awakening in England, sending out hundreds of preachers. This movement did not involve Rip Van Winkle.

1793-1900
THE BEGINNING OF MODERN MISSIONS: In 1793 William Carey sails for India, taking Christ to the Orient. Over the next century, thousands of missionaries are sent out, bringing Christianity to the world.

1960-1980
ELECTRONIC CHURCH: Television "churches" become prevalent as more and more preachers take to the air.

The Church grew extremely fast after the resurrection of Jesus. It began to organize when the Holy Spirit directed the 12 disciples to assign administrative jobs to other leaders so the apostles could devote themselves to prayer and preaching. (See Acts 6:1-7.) Through the years the organization called the Church grew and changed in many ways. Today there are many types of churches. They are organized in different ways, worship in different ways, and meet in different kinds of buildings. They have varying beliefs and practices. But all who trust in Jesus Christ are a part of the Church that Jesus started. And God continues to work through that Church.

ACTIVITY PIECE A2 by Dan Runyon and Paul Woods. Illustrated by Paul Turnbaugh. Portions adapted from *Young Teen Action,* Year III, © 1984 David C. Cook Publishing Co. © 1986 David C. Cook Publishing Co. Permission granted to reproduce for ministry use only—not for resale.

A SIMULATION
CHURCH MEETING

INSTRUCTIONS

Read the situation (below) and make sure everyone understands it.

Ask for five volunteers. Give one character role card to each volunteer. Allow volunteers a few minutes to study their roles. Remind them that they are supposed to disagree and that it is okay to argue heatedly. Encourage each of the volunteers to make at least three or four statements during the simulation. You might want Gloria Swanson (the old lady) to start with a statement about never having paid a pastor that much before.

SITUATION

An annual church meeting in January. Members are trying to decide whether or not they should raise the new pastor's salary. Pastor Thompson has been at the church since the summer. His wife works full-time at a clothing store in the next town. They have three kids: one an eighth-grader, one a high school sophomore, and the other a senior. Opinion on the raise is divided.

ACTIVITY PIECE B1 by Eric Potter
©1986 David C. Cook Publishing Co.
Permission granted to reproduce for ministry use only—not for resale.

Character Role Card:

Gloria Swanson

You are an elderly woman and have been a member since the church started many years ago. You are against the raise and argue: "We never paid a pastor that much before." You don't dislike Pastor Thompson, but you're not overly thrilled with him. The former pastor (Pastor Smith) was closer to your age and spent a lot of time with you and the other elderly members. You feel neglected by the new pastor. You also disapprove of Mrs. Thompson's job because you think she should stay at home and be a "pastor's wife."

Character Role Card:

Tanya Jackson

You are the church treasurer and are against the raise. You worry about the budget. If giving doesn't increase you don't know how you can afford the raise. You fear that you will have to cut back some other program to pay for it. You threaten the youth pastor that it may be in his department and hint that it may even be his job.

Character Role Card:

David Bird

You are the youth pastor and are for the raise. You argue that the pastor deserves a good salary because of his education and experience. You know what long hours he puts in. And you point out that his oldest kid will be going to college in the fall. Also, your wife works and you resent Gloria Swanson's implied criticism of the pastor's wife.

Character Role Card:

Steven McConnel

You are a businessman and influential church member. You are against the raise. You can't understand what the pastor does with all of his time—you think he's overpaid for the amount of work he does. You also believe he lives extravagantly: after all, he has two cars and one is an almost new station wagon. You accuse the youth pastor of supporting the raise only to increase his future prospects.

Character Role Card:

Lance Burkhart

You are a congregation member and close friend of Pastor Thompson. You are about the same age as he and have children about the same age as his. One of your kids is in college and you know how difficult it is to pay for it even on your salary. You know the pastor's salary and are amazed his family can survive on it. You know that the pastor's wife works out of necessity. You know that the pastor's family has four drivers and only two cars. You also know that McConnel bought a new Mercedes last month.

WORKING PART
— OR —
MONKEY WRENCH?

How smoothly do you run in your church "machine"?

1. What is your opinion of the pastor of your church (or class teacher, or youth pastor)?

2. Where do you think this attitude came from?

3. How does Hebrews 13:17 apply to your situation with this person?

4. Is there someone in this group (or church) who really bugs you? Why?

5. Is it the person's fault, or something beyond his or her control?

6. What does Romans 12:10 say to your relationship with this person?

7. Does our church offer any programs that you think are dumb, or a waste of time? If so, have you ever criticized them?

8. What positive suggestions can you make to improve those programs? To whom should you talk about your suggestion?

9. Look back over this sheet and pick out one area where you see you need to change. What one concrete thing can you do this week to help make this change?

Removing Sand from the Gears

Think about this: Whenever you see a problem, it may indicate that God thinks you can help solve that problem. Instead of criticizing or complaining, ask God what He wants you to do that will make a difference.

ACTIVITY PIECE B2 by Dan Runyon ©1986 David C. Cook Publishing Co. Permission granted to reproduce for ministry use only—not for resale.

Gilda Y. Groupie

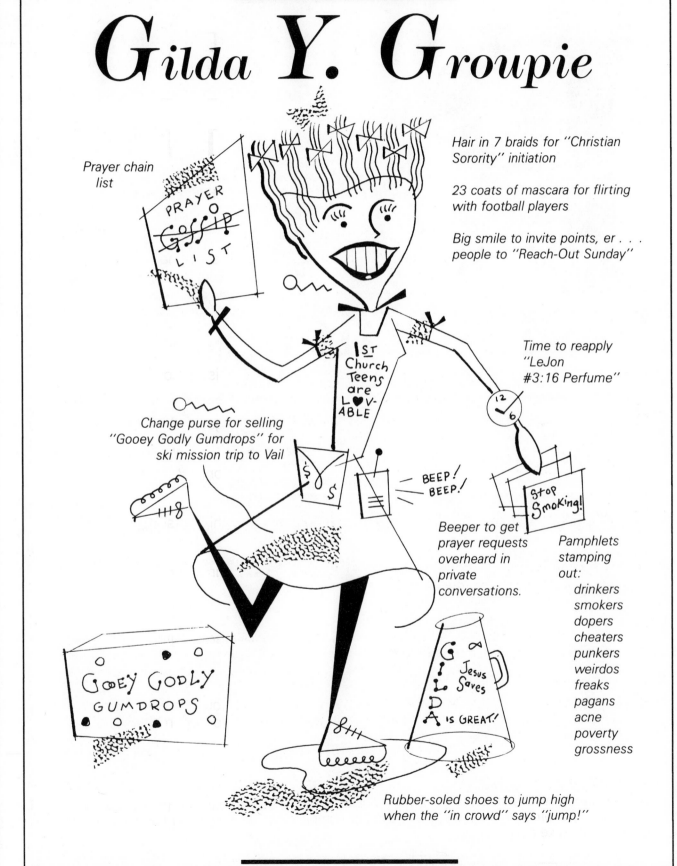

Prayer chain list

Hair in 7 braids for "Christian Sorority" initiation

23 coats of mascara for flirting with football players

Big smile to invite points, er . . . people to "Reach-Out Sunday"

Time to reapply "LeJon #3:16 Perfume"

Change purse for selling "Gooey Godly Gumdrops" for ski mission trip to Vail

PRAYER GOSSIP LIST

1st Church Teens are L♥V-ABLE

BEEP! BEEP!

Stop Smoking!

GOOEY GODLY GUMDROPS

G I L D A
Jesus Saves ∞ IS GREAT!

Beeper to get prayer requests overheard in private conversations.

Pamphlets stamping out:
drinkers
smokers
dopers
cheaters
punkers
weirdos
freaks
pagans
acne
poverty
grossness

Rubber-soled shoes to jump high when the "in crowd" says "jump!"

Illustration by Craig Yoe

ACTIVITY PIECE C1 by Bill Reif © 1986 David C. Cook Publishing Co. Permission granted to reproduce for ministry use only—not for resale.

PRESSURE INVENTORY

Instructions

The column on the left represents actions and attitudes that can exert negative pressure on a group. The column on the right lists positive actions and attitudes that can provide positive pressure. Match each negative pressure with its opposite positive response.

1. gossiping about people in the group

2. sitting only with select people

3. worrying about one's image

4. seeking to attract attention

5. making others feel left out

6. cutting others down

7. dropping one's friends when aggravated

8. looking to the group for approval

9. treating people differently at school than at church

10. worrying about not being liked

11. criticizing those who are growing spiritually

12. encouraging others to rebel

A. praying about people's problems and needs

B. being concerned about being a friend to others

C. seeking to serve

D. looking to God for approval

E. making others feel accepted

F. being excited for those who are excited about Christ

G. being consistent in one's friendships

H. sitting with someone who needs encouragement

I. worrying about Christ's image

J. sticking with friends through hard times

K. encouraging others to follow the adult leaders

L. making others feel special

ACTIVITY PIECE C2 by Bill Reif © 1986 David C. Cook Publishing Co. Permission granted to reproduce for ministry use only—not for resale.

7 ORDINARY · CHURCHES

Look up the Scriptures listed to discover each church's strengths and weaknesses. In your own words, write a brief description of each strength or weakness in the chart.

CHURCH	STRENGTHS	WEAKNESSES
The Church in Ephesus	Revelation 2:2, 3	Revelation 2:4
The Church in Smyrna	Revelation 2:9	none listed
The Church in Pergamum	Revelation 2:13	Revelation 2:14, 15
The Church in Thyatira	Revelation 2:19	Revelation 2:20
The Church in Sardis	Revelation 3:4	Revelation 3:1, 2
The Church in Philadelphia	Revelation 3:8, 10	none listed
The Church in Laodicea	none listed	Revelation 3:15-17

Look over the chart. Did any of the churches have the same weaknesses? The same strengths? What does this tell you about churches?

ACTIVITY PIECE D1 © 1986 David C. Cook Publishing Co. Permission granted to reproduce for ministry use only—not for resale.

Team Assignments

E Y E S

You are the only person who sees the original drawing. Your assignment is to look at the drawing carefully, and describe what you see. You may only whisper observations and directions to the MOUTH, who will speak them out loud for the HANDS to hear.

H A N D S

You are the only person who may use your hands. Your assignment is to draw the picture. You base your drawing on whatever instructions the MOUTH tells you. You cannot speak, and can use only one hand.

M O U T H

You are the only person who may speak out loud. Your assignment is to tell the HANDS what to draw. You base your instructions on the information the EYES (the only one who can see the original drawing) whispers to you.

F E E T

You are the only person who may use your legs and feet. Your assignment is to hold the paper steady for the HANDS to draw on. You cannot speak, and cannot use your hands or arms.

ACTIVITY PIECE E1 by Kent Lindberg © 1986 David C. Cook Publishing Co. Permission granted to reproduce for ministry use only—not for resale.

Team Drawing

The Thingamajig

ACTIVITY PIECE E2 by Kent Lindberg © 1986 David C. Cook Publishing Co. Permission granted to reproduce for ministry use only—not for resale.

Me and the Body

Looking at you and the youth group

1. Read I Corinthians 12:27-31.

2. Why do you think all Christians are not supposed to have the same gifts or be exactly the same?

3. Finish these phrases:
One thing special about me is . . .

Whether it shows or not, I am important to this group because . . .

4. Read I Corinthians 13. The "more excellent way" Paul mentions in I Corinthians 12:31 is the way of love. We have God's own love working through us.

5. Finish these phrases:
One way I show love for people in this group is . . .

Another way I could show love to them is . . .

ACTIVITY PIECE BR1 by Paul Boostrom © 1986 David C. Cook Publishing Co. Permission granted to reproduce for ministry use only—not for resale.

The "I Am" Survey

Finish the sentence by choosing one word from each line that best describes you.

Most of the time I am . . .

☐ Leader	☐ Follower	☐ Loner
☐ Talker	☐ Listener	☐ Outsider
☐ Steady	☐ Reliable	☐ Helpful
☐ Loyal	☐ Questioning	☐ Creative
☐ Believing	☐ Questioning	☐ Talkative
☐ Learning	☐ Content	☐ Curious

For each word you choose, tell how this quality can help the group.

ACTIVITY PIECE BR2 by Paul Boostrom © 1986 David C. Cook Publishing Co. Permission granted to reproduce for ministry use only—not for resale.

STARGAZER'S SCRIPT

A LOOK AT THE STARS—AND BEYOND

(Read slowly and softly, leaving pauses between sentences.)

Pick a star, any star. Watch it carefully, noticing its position in relation to the stars around it. Millions of miles away from you, this star shines a light. The rays you see left there long ago. They were bright there and still are. They are part of the testimony this star has made for ages.

Your star is brighter than some, isn't it? And not as bright as others. Notice the surrounding sky. You, too, are placed in a specific part of creation by a loving Creator, to give glory to Jesus Christ. Just like the star, the world surrounding you would be missing something without you.

But your star does what God planned, all the time. It has no choice. You do. You can refuse to be who God made you to be. You can try to be someone else. But you can be only a second-rate someone else. You can be the best YOU God ever made! Listen. Look at your star and listen:

He is the image of the invisible God, the firstborn over all creation. For by him all things were created: things in heaven and on earth, visible and invisible, whether thrones or powers or rulers or authorities; all things were created by him and for him. He is before all things, and in him all things hold together. And he is the head of the body, the church; he is the beginning and the firstborn from among the dead, so that in everything he might have the supremacy.
(Colossians 1:15-18)

Who is this about? There is no doubt. It is Jesus, the Christ, God the Son. Your star is no accident. Neither are you. The sky was not created for your star, but for Christ. You were not created for your pleasure, but for His.

Notice how large the universe is . . . how small you are. Yet the Lord God Almighty did not make you insignificant, nor did He make you a spectator. Listen to the Psalmist's words:

O Lord, our Lord, how majestic is your name in all the earth!
You have set your glory above the heavens.
When I consider your heavens,
    the work of your fingers,
    the moon and the stars,
    which you have set in place,
    what is man that you are mindful of him,
    the son of man that you care for him?
You made him a little lower than the heavenly beings
    and crowned him with glory and honor.
You made him ruler over the works of your hands;
    you put everything under his feet.
(Psalm 8:1, 3-6.)

You, too, are called to be shining His glory, actively doing what you can do best, telling the story of what God has done for you in Jesus Christ.

Go now to your night's sleep. Go silently. Thank the Lord for allowing you to be part of His plan, for making you important, for making you part of His forever family!

ACTIVITY PIECE BR 3 by Paul Boostrom © 1986 David C. Cook Publishing Co. Permission granted to reproduce for ministry use only—not for resale.